Emotional Labor
and Crisis Response

Emotional Labor
and Crisis Response
Working on the Razor's Edge

Sharon H. Mastracci
Mary E. Guy
Meredith A. Newman

Routledge
Taylor & Francis Group

LONDON AND NEW YORK

First published 2012 by M.E. Sharpe

Published 2015 by Routledge
2 Park Square, Milton Park, Abingdon, Oxon OX14 4RN
711 Third Avenue, New York, NY 10017, USA

Routledge is an imprint of the Taylor & Francis Group, an informa business

Library of Congress Cataloging-in-Publication Data

Mastracci, Sharon H., 1968–
  Emotional labor and crisis response : working on the razor's edge / by Sharon H. Mastracci,
Mary E. Guy, and Meredith A. Newman.
    p. cm.
  Includes bibliographical references and index.
  ISBN 978-0-7656-2518-2 (hardcover : alk. paper) — ISBN 978-0-7656-2519-9 (pbk. : alk. paper)
  1. Public service employment—United States—Psychological aspects. 2. Crisis
management—United States. I. Guy, Mary E. (Mary Ellen) II. Newman, Meredith A., 1949–
III. Title.

HD5713.6.U54M37 2011
363.34068′1—dc22   2011005568

ISBN 13: 9780765625199 (pbk)
ISBN 13: 9780765625182 (hbk)

I would not give a fig for the simplicity this side of complexity, but I would give my life for the simplicity on the other side of complexity.

—Oliver Wendell Holmes Sr.

Contents

Foreword

Janet V. Denhardt and Robert B. Denhardt

We take for granted in Western culture that we "think" with our mind and "feel" with our heart. With regard to our jobs, however, the prevailing norm is that we ought to rely on the former, using our cognitive and intellectual skills to perform our duties. Although some have decried the neglect of the heart or "soul" of public service, we have only begun to empirically explore the critical and essential role of emotion in public service work.

Emotional Labor in Crisis Response takes us many steps along that path by providing new and highly useful research based on the authors' previous work on emotional labor. Their previous book, *Emotional Labor: Putting the Service in Public Service*, challenged the mainstream assumption that cognition and reason are the primary bases for action in the public service. Instead, the authors argued that many, if not all, public servants are engaged in work that is significantly tied to emotional response and that some perform work that requires a very high degree of emotional engagement. Police officers, therapists, and emergency responders, for example, often work in highly emotionally charged situations that require them to regulate and manage their own emotional responses and set the emotional tone for others while completing their other tasks effectively and competently. They must then deal with the emotional aftermath in a manner that allows them to maintain their ability to respond with both compassion and skill in the future.

Emotional labor is not just emotional intelligence, though emotional intelligence would seem to be an important contributor. Emotional labor instead refers to the job requirement to recognize, understand, and regulate emotional exchanges with clients, citizens, and fellow public service workers as well. The authors define emotional labor as "the *effort within* oneself to conjure appropriate feelings or subdue inappropriate ones, and the effort to induce particular feelings in another person or stifle other feelings" (p. 28). To engage in emotional labor is not simply to act with emotions at the forefront, but to recognize the way in which emotions influence outcomes in terms of service. It is not simply a matter of having feelings or emotions on the job, but about the need to bring emotional skill and work to bear in order to meet the *requirements* of the job. "Workers must be able to suppress, control, or elicit their own and others' emotions as the job demands. In other words, their capacity to engage in, and their efficacy in, exerting emotional labor is essential to job performance" (p. 139).

But *Emotional Labor in Crisis Response* is not merely a reworking of the idea of emotional labor; it is instead based on new research designed to find out "how" emotional labor occurs and is experienced by public servants and the citizens with whom they work. In contrast to portraying the abstract world of administrative principles, the authors help us understand how things really are, how they are experienced in the most intense engagements between emotional laborers and the citizens they serve. How are "feelings" and "emotions" integrated into the requirements of the job? How do public servants experience the interplay of emotions that are essential to completing their work?

Specifically, the authors interview public servants whose work is "on the razor's edge"—that is, public servants who interact with citizens in the most extreme and emotionally laden situations. These jobs do not constitute the full range of public sector jobs that employ emotional labor. They are admittedly extreme; they constitute emotional labor "writ large." But it is from these examples that we can gain important insights into emotional labor as it engages public servants across the spectrum of public work.

The idea of emotional labor connects well with a stream of scholarship and, more important, with a strong impulse in the contemporary practice of public administration that recognizes that public service cannot be merely understood, nor at all practiced, based on objective reasoning alone. Indeed, as the authors note, a narrow focus on rational principles has "dehydrated" what gives public service meaning. While some jobs require a great deal of, or even predominantly emotional labor, we would suggest that in general emotional labor is becoming a more central and essential part of public service in all arenas. For example, public organizations are becoming increasingly open as they move to engage citizens in planning, policymaking, and the implementation of public programs and services. This age of citizen engagement has many benefits for all involved, but it can also involve a high degree of emotional labor. In dealing with government, citizens have emotions ranging from apathy and disinterest to anger or even rage. Emotional labor on the part of public servants is essential to forming trusting and collaborative relationships with and between citizens. We are increasingly asking public servants at all levels of the organization to create positive relationships with citizens, and by doing so, we are asking them to deal with and manage emotional issues and tasks.

How can we understand this work and prepare ourselves and others to do it well? The first step is to become aware that such labor exists and understand the role it plays. The second step, of course, is to learn and practice how to do it. This book gives us critical insights into both: it helps us to recognize the role of emotional labor and how it is practiced by giving us stories and lessons learned by front-line workers on the razor's edge. By studying the experiences of those who work in crisis situations, performing work that many of us can scarcely imagine, we can all learn how to become more skilled at emotional labor.

As we do so, we can more effectively blend theory and practice in our field. We found especially compelling the illustration at the beginning of Chapter 2 that contrasts the experience of a student in an MPA class learning about the fundamentals of public administration with the experience of a police detective leaning over a dead body and realizing that the horror of the situation has to be put aside because action needs to be taken. In part, what is occurring here is a difference between abstract management at the upper levels of public bureaucracies—the level at which most MPA instruction is pitched—and what happens at the street level. But more importantly, this passage illustrates the difference between the rational world of administrative theory and the emotion-laden world of administrative practice.

Administrative theory boasts a long tradition of emphasis on the rational; while there have been significant counterpoints to that tradition; it remains the mainstream point of view even today. As such, the rational model dominates public administration research and public administration education. But administrative practitioners, real public servants, even those graduated from schools teaching in the rational tradition, recognize that the world of rationality is itself bounded. Alongside rationality, practice engages the emotions, both those of public servants and the citizens they serve. To recognize the significant role of emotional work in public service, as this book does, is to begin to correct the imbalance between theory and practice that has been decried for so long.

As we noted at the beginning, we typically assume we "think" with our mind and "feel" with our heart. We emphasize the importance of cognition and thinking (with our brain) and deemphasize the role of the emotions and the heart, particularly when it comes to our jobs. We might do well to look instead at traditional Chinese philosophy, where the heart and mind are one: the Chinese character "xin" includes both thoughts and feelings. Based on this point of view, even the idea of taking emotion or feeling out of the thinking process makes no sense. In the Western world, however, we may need to be reminded of the essential role of the "heart" of public service. This book not only does so, but it teaches us how to practice emotional labor in public service based on the experience of those who know and practice it in times of crisis and personal need. These are lessons that can greatly benefit all public employees as we strive to foster an ever more effective, compassionate, responsive, and skilled public service. As Aristotle said, "Educating the mind without educating the heart is no education at all." This fascinating work takes us one step further to embrace both the mind and the heart in our education and scholarship for public service.

Preface

Cool heads, warm hearts. Isn't that what we want when public workers meet citizens? To achieve that combination requires not only cognitive labor but also emotional labor. The term "emotional labor" refers to the management of one's own feelings as well as those of the other in order to get the job done. It has multiple facets, ranging from authentic expression of the worker's emotional state to requiring workers to don masks and display an emotion that they do not actually feel, such as when they must seem nicer-than-nice or, conversely, tougher-than-tough. Successful performance depends on it.

Our management theories have always acknowledged the importance of cognitive work, but emotion work has been missing from our principles and proverbs. Although an essential element in public service delivery, the subject has been undertheorized, not well understood, and largely overlooked. To correct this, we have been plumbing the depths of emotional labor for most of a decade, introducing it into the lexicon of public administration theory and practice. In 2008 we published *Emotional Labor: Putting the* Service *in Public Service*. That book demonstrated that emotional labor is part of an occupation, not just something that a person brings to the job. The purpose and role of the position and job functions determine which employees will encounter emotional labor demands and what kind. We concluded, therefore, that employers should not simply take for granted that some people will "have it" and others will not.

Emotional labor is a requirement of nearly all jobs that require workers to engage with citizens. In fact, the management of feeling, though demanding, is positively related to job satisfaction, such that those who perform it are more likely than other employees to experience satisfaction with their work and to view their jobs as meaningful and worthwhile. It is the sweetener that flavors their workday and causes them to want to go to work the next day and the next.

From multiple perspectives—quality of work life, performance, service outcomes—management has an important role to play ensuring that the emotive aspects of the work are appreciated and acknowledged, that there are systems in place to reward its good performance, and that there are systems in place to address its downside. Our research makes it obvious that agencies should be screening, training, evaluating, and rewarding employees on the quality not just of their cognitive skills but also of their emotive skills and on their ability to mitigate overloads when the stress is too much.

The 2008 book was an effort to push the canon toward greater recognition of this dynamic in public service delivery. We defined it and brought it to the fore in public administration practice and scholarship. We argued, again and again, for the importance of emotional labor in public service, and we criticized its relative absence in public administration scholarship. Some people are listening. Many people are listening. *Emotional Labor: Putting the* Service *in Public Service* has been well received.

So why another book? Because the 2008 book launched far many more questions than it answered. Its positive reception told us that we were on to something; that we were at the beginning of a new discourse on public service, not a conclusion, and that conversation deserves ongoing attention.

In order to nudge the dialogue forward, this book probes the actual performance of emotional labor more deeply. We dig into it and ask "How is it done?" "What kind of self-talk goes on during its performance?" "How is it sandwiched into standard operating procedures?" "What does it feel like?" "How does it feel after the work is done?" "Who does it best?" "How does it fit into accountability standards?" "When is too much 'too much'?" And we go to extremes to find the answers in order to capture the simplicity on the other side of chaos. We query public servants working in dangerous, emotionally-intense crises every day: work that is on the razor's edge.

Like a .zip file, their workdays require a condensed, distilled version of the emotive skills required in more routine, orderly jobs. Responding to one emergency after another, they experience a panoply of emotional demands. What keeps them coming back? Why do they do this work? How do they do this work? They answer our questions, and we use their words to explicate the subject of this book.

Acknowledgments

This project reflects the help of many people. First, we would like to express our sincere gratitude to Harry Briggs of M.E. Sharpe, Inc., for his continued enthusiasm for our work. We're just wild about him.

We also are grateful to Heather Liska and Robert J. Liska, whose experiences as first responders informed their critique and helpful suggestions to an early draft. Their insights and perspective kept us on track and strengthened the final manuscript. Most important, we extend our heartfelt gratitude to all the responders who gave us their time, their recollections, and their insights. It is through their words that we understand the work of crisis responders and all the forces that barrage them as they help those in need. And we would be remiss not to thank Bess Seeley for the many hours of transcription, listening over and over to words spoken in echo-filled rooms, until they came to life in sentences and paragraphs. Thank you, all!

Emotional Labor
and Crisis Response

1

Emotional Labor as Public Good and the State as Harbor of Refuge

Illinois Interstate 294—the Tri State tollway—carves a long, flat arc around the city of Chicago, extending north to Wisconsin and east to the Indiana state line: seventy-eight miles in total. Unlike other products of the post–World War II surge in infrastructure development, the Tri State was not built anew but instead is a patchwork of new roads and old, with portions dating back to the 1920s. Nevertheless, the Tri State is one of the most heavily traveled highways in the United States, carrying more than 100,000 vehicles every day (IDOT 2009). The Mile-Long Bridge conveys eight lanes of the Tri State over the Des Plaines River, the Chicago Sanitary and Ship Canal, dozens of railroad tracks, and the United Parcel Service Midwest intermodal facility. At one end of the bridge, the northbound and southbound lanes split, leaving a gap of several feet.

In the wee hours of one cold February night, a truck driver—a husband, a father to three small children—was heading southbound on the Tri State and fell asleep as he approached the Mile-Long Bridge. He crashed through the median guardrail, through the gap between the lanes, and plunged to the ground. He was trapped inside his cab under the trailer. He was about ten miles from home. Emergency responders were dispatched to the site. A responding paramedic describes the scene:

> Basically I'm inside the cab holding the guy's hand . . . they're trying everything they can, . . . [but] this guy's pinned so bad and the problem was that the truck was kind of up on top of him here, so we were trying to figure out how we were going to make this work. But I'm looking at him, I see him going into shock and there's no way. I just know we're not going to get him out. I'm not telling *him* that.
>
> When I saw the way he was pinned in there and knowing the amount of weight we had on this truck, I knew it was going to be at least two, three hours before we could get him out of there. . . . I just knew it wasn't going

to happen. Again, I'm not telling him that. . . . I'm being positive: "We'll get you, we'll get you . . . we're working on this, we're working on that." I said, "Tell me some more about your family," and the whole time I'm holding his hand. I mean I'm not letting go of his hand. I'm holding his hand and just—cold to the touch. And then I can feel his hand getting colder and colder and he's getting *more pale . . .*

Tragically and beautifully, this story illustrates emotional labor on two fronts: eliciting a particular emotional state in another person and emotion regulation within oneself. Emotional labor is "the management of feeling to create a *publicly observable* facial and bodily display" that is necessary for doing the job (Hochschild 1983, p. 7, emphasis supplied). It requires workers to suppress their private feelings in order to show desirable work-related emotions (Guy, Newman, & Mastracci 2008). Emotional labor is an indispensable skill in roughly one-quarter to one-third of all occupations and in all street-level occupations in the public sector (Guy, Newman, & Mastracci 2008; Hochschild 1983; McCloskey 2008). Public servants who cannot manage their own or another's feelings fail to do their jobs, just as surely as the physical laborer who cannot lift or carry weight. Because emotional labor is fundamental to the job, it is also part of a worker's salary: "emotional labor is sold for a wage and . . . has exchange value" (Hochschild 1983, p. 7).

As fundamental as it is to public service, emotional labor is all but absent from job descriptions and performance evaluations (Mastracci, Newman, & Guy 2006). So how did this paramedic know what to do? What's more, *how* did he do it? How did he stay "positive" and keep himself from breaking down? How did he keep his face and voice from betraying what he knew—that rescue was impossible and that the truck driver would never see his wife, his children, again? The paramedic foresaw the outcome but focused on selected aspects of the truth. How did he do that? This paramedic was also a husband, a father; how did he resist thoughts of his own wife and child and employ the following emotion regulation strategies?

- Situation modification: efforts "to directly modify the situation so as to alter its emotional impact," as shown by the paramedic's commitment to stay positive and by his reassurances to the victim (*We'll get you, we'll get you . . . we're working on this, we're working on that*).
- Attention deployment: "How individuals direct their attention within a given situation in order to influence their emotions." This effort includes distraction (*Tell me some more about your family*) and focused concentration (*I'm inside the cab holding the guy's hand . . . I'm not letting go of his hand*).

- Response modulation: efforts to influence "physiological, experiential, or behavioral responding as directly as possible," which again is demonstrated by the paramedic's commitment to stay positive and hide what he knows (*it was going to be at least two, three hours before we could get him out of there*) from the victim (*I'm not telling* him *that*). (Gross & Thompson 2007, pp. 12, 13, 15)

The paramedic in this story also betrays his awareness that, in this situation, "telling" means not only speaking, but also communicating nonverbally via his tone of voice, facial expressions, and physical gestures. Where did this awareness come from? Are some people just born with it, or can it be learned? Hochschild suggests the latter when she observes that emotional labor is not "*merely* a facet of personality" (1979, p. 568, emphasis supplied). It is more than a personality trait; it is a skill that can be learned and honed. Studies in experimental psychology have demonstrated this repeatedly. We discuss them below as part of the "Why" of emotional labor.

Emotional Labor: What, How, and Why

The "What"

In our previous research on emotional labor, we sought to answer questions related to its definition, presence, and role in public service delivery (Guy & Newman 2004; Guy, Newman, & Mastracci 2008; Mastracci, Newman, & Guy 2006; Newman, Guy, & Mastracci 2009). We consulted linguistics in order to define it and consulted other professions in order to understand it in public service practice. In the process, we discovered several important dimensions of emotional labor. First, at varying levels of intensity, it plays a role in nearly all government jobs. Frontline workers deal with the day-to-day needs of an increasingly demanding public; management handles the inter- and intra-agency demands of subordinates and superiors on everything from budget and human resources to agency turf battles. Second, we found that the performance of emotional labor need not lead to burnout. Public servants are as energized by intense emotional labor demands as they are exhausted. The difference lies in how management and workers address the emotive labor demands of these jobs. This led us to a third conclusion: Emotional labor is part of an occupation, not simply something that a person brings to the job (or not). The characteristics of the job—its purpose and role in the organization, its demands and requirements—determine whether or not job holders will find themselves exerting emotional labor. This led to a fourth conclusion: Agencies can screen, train, retrain, and evaluate employees on the quality of emotional labor that they exercise on the job. But it is the rarest office that even recognizes the emotive demands on its workers, much less evaluates and compensates for them. Finally, we found public administration theory and scholarship to be woefully short in recognizing and examining this subject. It is undertheorized in public administration. Our earlier book was an effort to push the canon in that direction (Guy, Newman, & Mastracci 2008). We sought to define emotional labor and bring it to the fore in public administration practice and scholarship.

The "How"

Emotional labor requires workers to suppress, exaggerate, or otherwise manipulate their own and/or another's private feelings in order to comply with work-related display rules. Private-sector jobs demand it because it contributes to the bottom line (Hochschild 1983). Public service jobs require emotional labor because they involve working directly with people and, more crucially, because they target vulnerable populations or people in vulnerable situations. This is due to the nature of the services provided by government and the role of government as harbor of refuge. Both of these are discussed later in this chapter.

How public servants exerted emotional labor was beyond the scope of our earlier research. In this book, we take as given the presence of emotional labor in public service and investigate *how* it is done. How do public servants interpret unwritten "feeling rules," and how are they integrated into the execution of one's duties? We explore worker strategies and approaches to crisis situations. In an instant and faced with panicked and traumatized victims, how do workers size up a situation and decide how to proceed? How do they frame and define the situation? How do they establish trust and elicit cooperation? How do they perceive their roles as representatives of the state, yet also as fellow citizens working under extreme pressure? How do they use discretion in different situations? We further consider the ethical dimensions of exercising autonomy while also possessing the power of the state. In short, we seek a fuller understanding of emotional labor exerted by public servants as they face grave challenges. In the cover illustration of this book, men and women climb atop a towering razor blade and walk across its edge. We want to know how they walk across the razor's edge and, in terms of "self-care," how they keep their balance.

Crisis response is a uniquely fertile context within which to study the "how" of emotional labor. All crisis responders rely on their capacity to manage their own and/or others' emotions almost all of the time as part of their jobs. Crisis response is unique to public service because it is a public good. Furthermore, crisis response is purposefully *not* representative of all public service; indeed, we chose crisis response *because* it is an extreme type of public service.[1] Crisis responders exert emotional labor to a degree and intensity that few others do, and our respondents represent a range of occupations: domestic violence hotline workers, emergency medical staff, and department spokespersons who are the initial face of the organization and who address the public immediately after crises.

Our deliberate choice of high-intensity occupations is akin to the approach taken by Carol Gilligan in her pathbreaking book, *In a Different Voice* (1982). She studied the gendered nature of moral development by interviewing women considering abortion, which is obviously not "random" or "representative" of decisions a woman must make, but it is one that allowed her to capture the strategies and approaches that women take when making moral judgments. If there were any decision that would betray a woman's moral calculus, Gilligan hypothesized, considering abortion would definitely be it. Likewise, if there were any type of public service that would reveal workers' strategies and approaches to exercising emotional labor, crisis response is it. Both are time bound. A woman must act early in her pregnancy—after that, the decision is made for her by law and cannot be reversed. Similarly, in the case of sworn officers, crisis responders cannot choose *not* to act—to refuse to act is to violate their oath and fail to do their jobs.

A significant difference between ours and Gilligan's respondents involves the ability to anticipate. Unlike women facing the abortion decision, which for many is a once-in-a-lifetime situation, first responders confront crises as a regular part of their occupations. Despite all their preparation, however, unanticipated events occur. We asked crisis responders about their worst experiences, those in which they felt underprepared or unprepared and those that took them by surprise (Troxell 2008). Our objective was to elicit responses about their use of emotional labor in crisis response. (See Appendix A for a detailed discussion of our assumptions about respondents' abilities to articulate how they exert emotional labor.)

We interview public servants who work *on the razor's edge*. Our goal is to learn their strategies for handling emotionally intense situations, how they exercise discretion, how they understand the roles that they are expected to play, and how they fulfill those expectations. Working in crisis situations as a fundamental part of their jobs requires public servants to flex their emotional muscles all at once. We can capture numerous, varied facets of on-the-job emotional labor in an instant or a series of instants. And an accumulation of crisis events allows us to tap into the evolution of workers' strategies and approaches. We rely on respondents' recollections and observations of crises, the demands of their jobs, and how or whether their actions and reactions have developed over time.

The "Why": Emotion Regulation and Cognitive Performance

The premise that politics and administration are mutually exclusive set into motion decades of public administration research along two trajectories: good and bad, or rational/objective/scientific/good and illogical/subjective/ discursive/bad. To the extent that emotions were mentioned at all, they would certainly be in the second group. Much of mainstream public administration scholarship is founded in the so-called politics-administration dichotomy, an assumption that permits researchers to study administration in isolation from politics, ceteris paribus. This assumption silences emotional labor, which is a subtle but crucial aspect of the economy and a not-so-subtle and even more crucial component of public service (McCloskey 2008; Guy, Newman, & Mastracci 2008). What's more, the politics-administration dichotomy sets emotion and cognition at cross purposes.

Our 2008 book challenged the assumption of orthodox public administration theory that cognition and reason are the best, the most appropriate, the only underpinnings of decision making and action. This is an assumption rooted deeply in the scientific management origins of the discipline. We challenged the primacy of cognitive skills and abilities—the reification of "objectivity"—in a discipline that requires its practitioners to work closely with people on relational matters. Now, however, we know more about the relationship between emotion and cognition. First, we have learned that, even among philosophers, the relationship between emotion and reason is not straightforward, as if emotions were, in Rietti's words, "random inclinations distorting the clean operations of practical reason." Even Enlightenment philosophers, including "the usual suspects, Hume, Descartes, and the emotivists tend to turn out, on closer inspection, to have rather more sophisticated accounts [of the relationship between emotion and reason] than they are often credited with." Philosophers of the twentieth and twenty-first centuries continue to deconstruct the "cognitivist paradigm" (Rietti 2009, pp. 68–69) and posit cognition in emotionality and emotion in cognition. Second, we have learned that not only are emotion and cognition linked, but emotion regulation affects cognitive function.

One of the earliest experiments on the relationship between emotion and cognition revealed the "cognitive consequences" of emotion regulation and concluded that "emotion suppression impaired memory for information encountered while individuals inhibited ongoing emotion-expressive behavior" (Richards & Gross 1999, p. 1042). The de rigueur method of eliciting emotion in experimental psychology is to show participants images—moving or still—that depict surgeries, traffic accidents, and other "disgust-inducing" and "gruesome" situations (Dunn, Billotti, Murphy, & Dalgleish 2009; Schartau,

Dalgleish, & Dunn 2009; Scheibe & Blanchard-Fields 2009, p. 217; Schmeichel 2007; Schmeichel, Volokhov, & Demaree 2008). To gauge the effect of emotion regulation on cognitive function, participants are instructed to exaggerate or suppress felt emotions and complete various tests of cognitive function, usually something involving working memory (Dunn et al. 2009; Schartau et al. 2009; Scheibe & Blanchard-Fields 2009; Schmeichel 2007; Schmeichel et al. 2008). Test results from these participants are then compared to those of participants who also viewed emotion-eliciting images but received no emotion-regulation instructions.

Schmeichel (2007, p. 251, emphasis supplied) focuses on how people ration a given amount of energy available to control emotion and perform cognitive tasks. The conclusion is that "although the executive control of memory and the executive control of emotion may emanate from distinct areas of the brain . . . performing *one* of these temporarily impaired the performance of the *other*." Moreover, emotion control at one point in time impeded subsequent attempts at emotion control. Dunn et al. (2009, p. 772) conclude that "the longer-term consequences of emotion suppression are an ongoing dampening of reactivity, reduced emotional response to positive material [and] reduced memory of the material encoded." While we speculated on the cumulative impact of emotional labor (see our process models in Guy, Newman, & Mastracci 2008, pp. 183–185), the corrosive effect of emotional labor on cognitive function has been demonstrated in the laboratory.

To determine whether emotion regulation and cognitive capacity vary together, Schmeichel et al. (2008, p. 1537) pretested participants' working memory before subjecting them to emotion-inducing imagery. They concluded that people at higher levels of cognitive capacity are more adept at controlling their emotional expressions. But they could not sort out the direction of causality: "it is also possible that, rather than working memory facilitating emotion regulation, good emotion regulation facilitates working memory." To determine whether emotion regulation exacts similar cognitive costs for people of varying ages, Scheibe and Blanchard-Fields (2009) compared the working memory performance of younger adults and older adults as they engaged in a specific type of emotion regulation—suppression—on a specific type of emotion—disgust; the researchers found that older adults perform better.

All these studies show that it is not the *experience* of emotion that impairs cognitive function, but rather the *regulation* (suppression or exaggeration) of it that impairs cognitive function. In other words, being emotional does not distort "the clean operations of practical reason" (Rietti 2009, p. 68); trying *not* to be emotional does.

Given the emotional labor burden on public servants, it is clear that to ignore emotional labor and focus on knowledge, skills, and abilities (KSAs), standard operating procedures (SOPs), or other ostensibly straightforward aspects of work performance is to get only part of the story. Worse, ignoring emotional labor demands on workers misses the interrelated aspects of public service work, both relational and technical. This oversight can have important consequences in the case of crisis response. For example, the emergency medical technician (EMT) must submit a report after the team returns to the station and therefore must rely on memory for details of the call. That same EMT must suppress feelings of anger, alarm, disgust, or fear in order to respond to an incident and engage in the myriad highly technical tasks that must be performed. Details are not only important for the case itself, but are part of ongoing learning and may shape protocols and procedures for future incidents. Finally, crisis responders' incident reports are a part of the public record, and it is not unheard of for first responders to be implicated in wrongful death lawsuits, making their record keeping crucial for personal and institutional liability. The cost of failure is high, particularly because of the nature of the public goods and services they provide and the concept of the harbor of refuge. For Hochschild's (1983) flight attendants, emotional labor missteps could have resulted in unhappy customers and potentially lost sales. The effects of failing to appreciate and understand the role of emotional labor in public service—particularly in crisis response—are more nuanced. In our opening story, had the paramedic not done what he did, the team still would have "done all they could do" and the truck driver still would have died. But this would not have happened:

> He gave me a message and so I went and told his wife. . . . I went to the wake . . . and then I pulled the wife aside and I introduced myself and I said I was with your husband holding his hand until the very end . . . he talked about how much he loves you and the kids and that's all he talked about and I just want you to know that . . . she was very thankful.

When there is no bottom line, as is the case in public service, it is the performance that counts. If emotional labor was important to understanding the service economy, as Hochschild (1983) showed, then it is infinitely more important in the context of public service. The effect of emotion regulation on cognition affects the breadth of technical and emotional skills employed by crisis responders and all public servants. To understand it is to truly understand how they do their jobs. It is the "how" to which this book is devoted.

The rest of this chapter is as follows: First, we define public goods and services, which are government's responsibility to produce and provide. The benefits of public goods and services—in this case, the benefits of crisis response—accrue to everyone. Their absence hurts everyone. Emotional labor is essential to the delivery of public services, but government reform efforts increasingly treat public goods and services like those of the private sector. Not only does this obscure the importance of emotional labor, but reform efforts emphasizing efficiency and cost can result in bad governance. We refer to recent welfare reforms to underscore the dangers of treating public services as though they were of the private sector. Public services are not private services and governments do not operate like businesses.

Second, we discuss the concept of the harbor of refuge. The state is granted broad authority by citizens to provide services that are not provided elsewhere—public goods—and to serve particularly vulnerable populations. For some populations—the most vulnerable, whether due to an inability to pay or due to an accident or crisis—and for some services like crisis response or law enforcement, government is the sole provider and/or provider of last resort. Both points—the nature of public goods and services, and the state as harbor of refuge—are meant to underscore the importance of understanding emotional labor. It is fundamental to the delivery of public goods and to serving the hardest to serve. If emotional labor is important to understand for a firm's bottom line, as Hochschild and others argue, then it is even more important to understand when there is no bottom line, as in the case of public goods and services.

The Role of the State: Providing Public Goods and Services

Every student in Economics 101 learns a definition of the field something along these lines: "Economics is the study of what to produce, how much to produce, and who gets it." Though simple, this statement actually covers a lot of ground. Resources are scarce, so choosing what to produce is a matter of determining where else you might spend your time and energy and settling on the product that will accrue the most on your investment. When circumstances change, you shift from one enterprise to a more lucrative one. Similarly, you choose how much to produce by determining the point at which it does not pay for you to spend any more time or energy in production, and you stop there. You can decide to cut back or expand if prices of the materials that you use in production change or if new developments allow you to charge a higher price. Finally, the "who gets it" question involves a choice of allocation mechanisms. Most goods and services are "normal" and allocated according to price: If you pay for it, you get it. If you don't, you don't. Dog food, beer, clothing, oil changes, bananas, manicures, air travel are but a few examples of normal goods and services.

Adam Smith (1776/1991) posited that people would get all the goods and services that they ever wanted and needed if each of them simply pursued their self-interest. The unseen hand would deliver everything to everyone if the process were free to operate. Smith's "invisible hand" metaphor endures: Two centuries later, Milton Friedman argued in *Capitalism and Freedom* (1962) that everyone is better off when each of us is free to choose what and how much to produce and consume, at prices deemed fair by each party, without interference from government. "Market failures" happen when goods and services that are demanded are not produced or when the price mechanism fails to satisfactorily allocate them.

Most public goods are due to market failures. Oftentimes, these are goods and services that no single producer can make enough profit by producing. They are beneficial to society, however, and are considered important to produce and provide anyway. VHS tapes are no longer profitable, but VHS tapes are not considered public goods that ought to be produced no matter what. Automakers try to cut costs as much as possible, but seat belts and air bags must be installed in every car because government says so—seat belts and air bags make everyone safer. Governments enact and enforce safety regulations such as these because consumer protection is a public good that no single firm would voluntarily provide—the costs of public goods and services are clear but their benefits are diffuse, difficult to measure, and impossible to price. "Because public goods such as roads and schools benefit society more than any individual or business, such investment would not have been adequately undertaken by private firms" (Madrick 2009, pp. 58–59).

For example, airlines are private-sector enterprises and all airlines need runways. But no single airline would incur the costs of building its own because it could not charge prices high enough to recoup its investment. It would not be able to compete with other airlines that would not need to cover such costs. Runways and airports are common resources, as is the service of managing air traffic. No single airline would allow another to manage takeoffs and landings: If United Airlines were in charge, it would let its own planes take off and land first, making its competitors wait. Airports, runways, and air traffic control, therefore, are public services provided by government. Creating and enforcing regulations are public services, as well. Airport security is a service that was provided by private contractors until September 11, 2001, after which time it was felt that government ought to assume responsibility for the task directly. Why? Because public servants lack a profit motive and are therefore deemed more trustworthy to provide such a critical service. Public services cannot be treated like normal goods, and the shift from private contractors to the Transportation Security Administration (TSA) provides an example. When it comes to national security, government should provide public goods and services, not the private sector.

Closer to the ground, law enforcement is provided by government as a public service. As a matter of principle, American society does not leave public safety only to those who can pay for it. A general sense of security accrues to all by prosecuting crimes and deterring potential crimes. Government cannot decide how much law enforcement service to provide based on the opportunity costs of the necessary personnel and equipment. Nor can government move these scarce resources to other, more lucrative, enterprises. In the absence of prices, the idea of a "lucrative" endeavor or a "return on investment" of resources imperfectly applies to the production and provision of public services. As Stivers notes, "This [free-market] model fits poorly into the public sector, where much of what is done is the result of market failure and many government services cannot be freely rejected" (2008, p. 106).

It is a mistake to treat public services like private goods, but that is precisely what happens when the rules of free markets are applied to serving the public. The rules of free markets require goods and services to be valued quantitatively. The value of a private good is its price. Public services are, at best, imperfectly priced. In the absence of prices, government cannot track revenues for the services that it provides. But costs are always knowable. Unlike private businesses, therefore, public services are governed by only half of the cost/revenue equation. Any cost-benefit analyses are imprecise and based on assumptions. When costs are easily calculated but benefits are difficult to quantify, everything seems expensive. So government always seems to operate inefficiently. If governments charged a fee for public services—even a heavily subsidized one—there would remain some citizens who cannot pay. Is it acceptable for government to withhold services from those who cannot pay? Imposing market principles on public services is problematic on a number of levels, but this has not prevented free-market ideologues from promising competitive market efficiencies and cost savings if only government would run like business. But if for-profit firms do not provide certain services because it is not in their fiduciary interest to do so, how can public services be provided as if they were normal goods? What is more, the definition of a private good is fluid and political. Various social safety net programs support the elderly, poor, disabled, single parents with young children, and the unemployed, but they also support AIG, Merrill Lynch, Lehman Brothers, Chrysler, and General Motors. Suddenly, the Federal Emergency Management Agency and the Department of the Treasury are twin emergency response agencies assigned to natural and not-so-natural disasters, respectively.

Taxpayers increasingly demand tangible returns on their investments. This creates incentives for government to overlook some citizens' best interests and ignore others who are most in need. For example, after passage of welfare reform legislation in 1996, states pointed toward declining welfare rolls as evidence of its effectiveness. Critics of welfare reform, however, accused states of placing people into any job in order to claim success. Workfare "satisfies both politicians and administrators. The former see the political benefits of headline-grabbing reductions in welfare rolls, while the latter seek the administrative benefits of a low-cost, outcomes-driven system" (Peck & Theodore 2002, p. 123). Given the incentives created by the gauge used to determine success, neither politicians nor administrators were motivated to consider the consequences for erstwhile welfare recipients. Although reform required them to "transition rapidly into the labor market . . . many welfare participants have not fared well in the competition for jobs because they face multiple barriers to employment," including lacking basic skills training, lack of transportation, insufficient child-care resources, and illiteracy (Blumenberg 2002, p. 314). Many men and women were placed in jobs and therefore considered success stories, but they could not stay employed; after they were off the welfare rolls and out of the system, they became invisible and were on their own.

What was the goal of welfare reform? Reducing the number of people receiving welfare or mitigating inequality? The two are not the same: The former is countable; the latter resists quantification. The former generates political capital for use in reelection campaigns; the latter takes time and manifests in various ways. The former is used as a proxy for the latter, even though such assumptions are hardly ever made explicit in analysis. Bryan (2005, p. 610) concludes, "The perception that the 1996 welfare reforms have been successful . . . rests on the faulty assumption that smaller welfare rolls imply reduced poverty and more gainful employment." But neither of these outcomes obtained. Even worse, Evelyn Brodkin (2007, p. 9) finds that the zeitgeist of market-based welfare reforms

> created an organizational environment that virtually gave free rein to discretionary practices that could produce caseload decline no matter how it was achieved, that is, even by tangling people in red tape, discouraging participation irrespective of need, creating excessive or misapplied proceduralism, and other forms of bureaucratic malfeasance, discouragement, and indifference.

Reducing laudable policy goals—breaking the poverty cycle and instituting a culture of work—to something countable like the number of welfare recipients can and has hurt the very people that the policy is meant to help. Similar consequences have arisen from efforts to reform public housing. For instance, fewer public housing units do not necessarily indicate declining demand for them (Crump 2003).

Quantification is not inherently bad, but its limitations are glossed over while its accuracy and objectivity are grossly overstated. Careless quantification calls to mind the metaphor about the drunk who lost his keys: He looks where the lamppost illuminates the sidewalk because that is where he can see. Using the number of welfare recipients—something we can see or count—as a proxy for economic inequality—something we cannot see or count—does not help us find our keys, either. Using market theory to answer questions about public goods and services is similarly fruitless. But repeated use of market-based methods to examine public service has transformed the lamppost approach from mistake to mainstream.

Careless quantification also fosters lazy analysis and leads one to overlook the elemental nature of public goods: Their value is not meted out in markets. Demand and supply curves do not intersect and settle on an equilibrium price and quantity. But we are continually asked to concoct imaginary prices for public goods in order to calculate imaginary revenues, which are compared to real costs as if public goods were private. Government is increasingly exposed to the "discipline of the market" through "reinvention" and pressured to prioritize efficiency over effectiveness. Prioritizing efficiency over effectiveness means that economic theory dictates decision making, replacing principles of public service. Maximizing the effectiveness of public services is replaced by minimizing costs of those services as a guiding principle for administration. Again, the two are not the same: Efficiency does not imply effectiveness.

Government has shifted from maximizing effectiveness (maximizing benefits to the greatest number of people) to maximizing efficiency (minimizing costs). Measuring effectiveness is precluded by the inability to gauge benefits, and measuring efficiency is precluded by the lack of revenues. The performance measurement movement has been somewhat successful in quantifying some aspects of providing public goods, but those measures will never be as clear as price is to determine value. Lacking a clear concept of price and therefore revenue, the public sector cuts expenditures without guidance on when to stop. The rationale seems to be that if costs are driven down further and further, then efficiency must follow. But government cannot operate according to free market principles because public goods and services are, by definition, exceptions to free market processes.

The Contested State

The role of the state is to protect and ensure citizens' freedom. From what? To do what? Camilla Stivers describes the minimalist view of the role of government—Leviathan—à la Thomas Hobbes: "Freedom is freedom from state interference other than whatever is necessary to keep us secure. Beyond that, Leviathan should keep quiet" (2008, p. 107).

Similarly, political philosopher Robert Nozick (1974) argues that groups and individuals should be free to seek their own self-fulfillment. Government should remain in the background and serve as "night watchman," interfering only when necessary. Pursuit of self-interest ultimately satisfies the interests of the whole, because latent interests are expressed and represented as well (Truman 1951). This is the same worldview as Adam Smith's unseen hand—that unfettered pursuit of individual interests in a marketplace of ideas ultimately benefits everyone. As "night watchman," our national government would secure its borders to preserve national security, print money, reinforce the rule of law, and provide legal structure for contracts and stable economic activity, but perhaps little else. State governments might construct and maintain roads, highways, bridges, and prisons; and local government might provide public education and public safety. This may be what libertarians and pluralists feel that the state "ought" to be, but is it? They and their partisans advocate a limited role for government and claim it to be the intent of the Founders, but their ideal state does not now depict the United States of America. "The romantic view of the limited role of government in America's economic history in the 1800s is simply wrong," Jeff Madrick (2009, p. 25) declares:

> Government policies, when they were most effective, were experimental and often bold, changed pragmatically with the times, and were not beholden to an ideology even in the time of Adam Smith's great popularity under Jefferson. In early America, the national government protected civil and property rights, set rules, did indeed have a tax policy of substantial tariffs, and had serious control over the nation's economy through its often radical land policies.

In their groundbreaking theoretical treatise on government and social structure, Evans, Rueschemeyer, and Skocpol (1985) expand the definition of "the state" and observe that the American state is an idea, an entity beyond its political boundaries. Accordingly, "market failures" and the "night watchman" have proven to be fluid concepts, allowing government's role to ebb and flow in response to citizen demands. And the demand has been for a broad, active government, perhaps most easily observed at the national level.

The immense institutions lining the mall in Washington D.C. symbolize the scale and scope of American government. Construction of these grand icons began as early as 1836 with the Department of the Treasury building. Like the Treasury building, many early national institutions were built in the Greek Revival style to reinforce the democratic ideals of ancient Greece throughout the young nation. In addition to these outward signs of large national government, the earliest welfare-state policy was enacted even before the establishment of the union itself. To increase enlistments for the Revolutionary War, the Continental Congress provided pensions for disabled soldiers. Federal government continued its support of veterans of the War of 1812, the Mexican-American War, and the Civil War. Disabled veterans' benefits were extended to survivors as early as the Civil War (Skocpol 1992). Stepping in to provide public services has been the role of the United States from its founding. Against this backdrop, the social safety net is not an aberration from a minimalist ideal (Krugman 2007), nor was it born anew in the twentieth century under the New Deal. It is the norm.

The citizenry grants power to the state to create and enforce policies ensuring worker protection and consumer protection, minimum wages, maximum hours, building codes, and standardization for everything from weights and measures to food labels and nutritional claims. Governments at all levels decide who can and cannot drive, marry, travel internationally, own weapons, enter into contracts, drink alcohol and smoke cigarettes, be tried for a crime, buy Sudafed, and serve on juries. Licensing governs a range of professional workers including accountants, barbers, dentists, lawyers, plumbers, nurses, and real estate agents. Government policies at all levels further determine the appropriate content for television and radio at different times of day, where and when you can park your car, how loud your music can be, what and where you can build, and what constitutes decent and indecent exposure. Laws also exist to outlaw truancy, child neglect, domestic violence, animal abuse and neglect, and yelling "fire" in a public place. Persons convicted of certain crimes are subject to further social regulations. For instance, convicted sexual assailants of children cannot live within a certain distance of schools, cannot hold jobs or volunteer positions involving interaction with children, and cannot pass out candy on Halloween. The public/private dichotomy is an obvious fiction. The public grants the authority to federal, state, and local governments to address a wide range of issues, especially in times of crisis. We demand the state to "do something"—to respond, to make things right.

The Harbor of Refuge

On the high seas, a harbor of refuge is known to be open to any vessel in distress requiring assistance, regardless of the flag it flies or the doctrines of its native country. Likewise, whether or not we support the current administration or have the ability to pay, we expect the government to respond when tragedy strikes. Crisis response is a public service. Furthermore, the state is expected to provide services regardless of citizens' ability to pay. For some citizens, the price mechanism of allocation fails, and for some services, it is considered highly inappropriate to even suggest that a price be charged. Current cultural norms prohibit charging prices for suicide or domestic violence hotline services, emergency room triage, and police and fire services. Advocates of universal health care want to eliminate the current allocation mechanism—price—and establish health care as a public good. Fees for some rescue services have been charged to victims if they are found liable for the situation. For example, emergency services can charge skiers or hikers needing rescue after going into off-limits parts of a park or otherwise not following the rules. Such fees are rare, however, and remain controversial.

Summary: Let's Set Sail

In the next chapter, we define emotional labor and set it apart from three main streams of public administration research: public service motivation, leadership, and emotional intelligence. After discussing public service scholarship, we turn our attention to practice. What is the status of emotional labor in the study of practice? In Chapter 3, we consider the implications of this new way of looking at public sector work on human capital management. In Chapters 4 through 7 we examine different aspects of public service that involve emotional labor. Jobs in crisis response face different expectations from different audiences: agency spokespersons address the public at large while first responders work directly with victims in acute crisis. Each involves different emotive skills.

Chapter 4 examines the immediate postcrisis response from the agency point of view. In the wake of tragedy, the public must believe the state to be trustworthy and competent. In Chapter 5, we examine the role of the individual as a representative of the state. By definition, public servants are not private citizens. Their actions are the agency's actions. How do they convince a citizen of the agency's responsiveness and accountability through their words and actions? Do they convince themselves first? In Chapter 6, we further plumb the tension between worker and job, and we ask public servants about the expectations that they face related to their roles as public servants: how is their power made legitimate? The individual is at once a representative of an agency as well as of an occupation. Chapter 7 is devoted to the tension between the impulse to eliminate ambiguity and the need to exercise discretion through extensive standard operating procedures and the inevitability, and desirability, of discretion on the part of crisis responders. This chapter addresses public servants as decision makers. We ask them whether, and if so how, the situation dictates strategy. How do they assess circumstance and how do they decide to act in one way or another? How does this happen in a split second and how have their strategies changed over time?

In the final chapter, Chapter 8, we summarize our findings, interpret their implications for public service, and look for new ways to examine emotional labor further. We discuss recent developments in organizational psychology of what have been called "crucial conversations." These relate directly to our arguments that emotional labor must be recognized and considered in workplace contexts. To exaggerate the point, the authors of *Crucial Conversations* describe a silence-to-violence cycle in which silence is the enforced norm until it is no longer tenable and violence—of words or, tragically, deeds—results. This cycle relates to emotional labor because, for its downside, silence means avoidance: avoiding crucial conversations, mismanaged emotions, and mismanaged emotion regulation. Sometimes external events trigger an end to the silence stage; other times employees can no longer accept the norm of silence imposed through organizational norms, respect for authority, or maintaining the status quo. It is important for administrators to overcome the lack of information and training in regard to emotion regulation. Rather than lose talented people to the downside of emotional labor, burnout, we seek to raise awareness of the normalcy of emotional reactions on the job and to devise strategies for anticipating and overcoming them.

Chronically overlooked stress can erupt into workplace confrontations, not conversations. The violence cycle begins with words and deeds intended to provoke. Workplaces that fail to reward those skilled in emotion work and that fail to deal with its stressful aspects risk the loss of trained, competent workers. And public administration scholarship that fails to appreciate emotional labor is primed for a metamorphosis of its own, an evolution, a cycle ushering in new ideas. This book is a part of that forward momentum.

Note

1. One big difference between crisis response units and other public service agencies is in their organizational forms. Crisis response entities work best in a command-and-control structure. In a crisis, rules need to be clear and chains of command must be followed. But not all public services require this degree of strict hierarchy. Structure, rules, and hierarchies manifest differently in organizations of different size and mission.

2

A Blind Spot in Public Administration Theory . . . But Not in Practice (*still*)

Imagine a student in a Master of Public Administration (MPA) degree program. He has worked in law enforcement for a few years and wants to be considered for promotion so he advances his education in order to make himself eligible for promotion up the ranks. Tonight's class is on the fundamentals of public administration. He reads about the science of administration and the will of the people, about efficiency and bureaucratic principles and divisions of labor and performance measures. He reads case studies about toxic waste dumps and mine disasters and competing models of policy implementation. Now imagine this student alongside one of our respondents, a police detective, who shares this story:

> So this is the situation: The gentleman was dead on the floor, but his dog had eaten the whole side of his face . . . and then you had normal face on the other side . . . there are things that you see and you put away for later to look at [because] you recognize as you're there, "I'm the only one here that can deal with this" and so I need to put that aside, whatever horror I'm feeling, and proceed with what I've been trained to do, which is to take the report, pass it to investigations, make the appropriate calls or whatever . . . those officers who do better take that horror that they've seen and look at it later, either with someone or by themselves in some self-talk or talking with a colleague.

What could our MPA student have learned that would prepare him for anything like the above situation? Our respondents repeatedly reported that their knowledge comes straight from experience; has scholarship nothing to add? Although public administration scholarship does not "see" emotional labor, or is nearsighted at best, the same cannot be said of public administration practice. In our interviews, for example, practitioners acknowledged the presence and importance of emotional labor as soon as we broached the subject. If scholarship is to inform practice and retain its relevance to public servants, we have some catching up to do. For example, what does it take to suppress emotion and then grapple with submerged feelings after the fact? Suppressing one's own horror while proceeding to perform the job is only one of many necessities of emotional labor. We discuss this in more detail after describing emotional labor in general. Its presence and practice, and its importance to delivering public services and how it challenges mainstream theory, were discussed in Chapter 1. While it does not defy measurement entirely, it poses problems for researchers who expect explicit indicators that measure deeply relational public service.

The difficulty in gauging emotional labor, as compared to measuring cognitive proficiency and physical fitness, has caused it to be largely overlooked by those interested in studying public service. As Denhardt and Denhardt argue, "There's no scientific answer to the most difficult problems that leaders face, and those problems are not amenable to solutions sought through the application of rational analytic techniques" (2005, p. 10). So it is with emotional labor. Public administration scholarship and practice have acknowledged the role of emotion in management, but only within the broader parameters outlined by studies of motivation, leadership, and emotional intelligence.

Our research on emotional labor in public service is indebted to these studies, for they illuminate the human side of public administration. But a blind spot remains. Capturing the "effort within" resists quantification, and in Chapter 1 we articulated the dangers of quantifying qualitative ideas carelessly. We used welfare reform as an example. Its qualitative nature led human resource and public performance scholarship to overlook emotional labor, rendering it invisible.

The literature has developed a sophisticated library of theoretical approaches that help us understand the essence of contracted services, constraints on collective action, challenges to democratic theory, and the construction of networks. Organization theory helps us understand how to bring diverse individuals together to achieve a mission that none, working singly, can achieve. Models of organization behavior help us understand the dynamics of interpersonal interactions and group performance. Organization development boosts our knowledge of how to achieve each worker's potential and how to harness the strengths of the group to achieve the goals of the organization. But none of these approaches informs us about the emotive exchange between worker and citizen.

The focus on principles and proverbs of "how to manage" has dehydrated what public service is all about. Overlooked is the appreciation for the juice or the spark that gives meaning to public service jobs. In interview after interview, responders told us that the emotional aspects of their jobs are what give meaning to their work. Knowing they made a difference in someone's life gives them reason to return to work the next day and face what, again, may be a challenging task.

The most intense—and most unscripted—point of contact between citizens and the state occurs when first responders encounter citizens when their lives have been turned upside down by storms, wrecks, fires, floods, earthquakes, crimes, or explosions. During these interactions, emotions are on the razor's edge. Split-second decisions are a must. The work is cognitive, often physical, and always emotional. Each interaction is compressed—a distilled, concentrated version of a usual workday exchange. Standing medical orders and standard operating procedures standardize processes, but the actual behaviors can never be totally scripted. Exigencies of the moment rule. This leaves action to the discretion of the worker, and the cumulative effect of emotional labor takes its toll, as described by one firefighter:

> I always say, well, since I have to work, this is what I want to do. It's a great job. It's gratifying. It's also a wake-up call a lot of times. I've led a wonderful life. I was sheltered by my parents and went to private school and had a great childhood. I have nothing to complain about. I've never witnessed, walked into the houses, and seen the decrepit conditions that I've seen in the last ten years before I got on the fire department. It has certainly rounded out my view of the world. That's probably something that I didn't expect to take away from the job that I do. I'm certainly a lot more aware of the potential for tragedy. It worries me a lot more in my own personal life. That's a negative about the job. Sometimes ignorance is bliss. And I'm not ignorant about anything anymore.

Emotional Labor: What It Is *Not*

It is helpful to set parameters around this intangible, invisible work behavior. To begin, we explain what it is not. First comes the familiar term "labor," which refers to work that is performed on the job in order to fulfill employment duties. There are three kinds of labor: physical, cognitive, and emotional. Physical labor involves, for instance, hauling, lifting, and shifting tangible objects. It requires physical exertion. A worker's aptitude for it can be tested and his performance can be measured and compared to someone else's. If a job requires physical labor, a supervisor can assess immediately—or if not immediately, then at least directly—whether the job has been done or not because the outcomes are visible.

Similarly, intellectual prowess can be tested in order to screen for qualified applicants. Intelligence tests, academic degrees, and course transcripts are used to assess—or to approximate—an applicant's ability to perform cognitive tasks. Unlike physical labor, its performance is intangible—the supervisor does not see the worker think—but the results are fairly straightforward. Knowledge work is quantifiable in terms of applications processed, cases resolved, reports written, and analyses conducted.

Emotional labor is misunderstood in comparison to these other two kinds of labor because an applicant's skill at performing it defies job-screening exams, the emotions are often invisible, and its effect on outcomes is indirect and not necessarily immediate. Successful performance facilitates human interaction, enabling a positive exchange between citizen and state. But it is the actual result of the exchange that is noted as the outcome, rather than the route by which the outcome was achieved. For example, the comments below demonstrate how emotional labor pays off in criminal investigations. A victim services coordinator who works in a city police department describes the work of victim advocates:

> Our job is to provide support, information, and referrals to victims of crime or personal tragedy and to ensure that their rights under the law are being afforded to them . . . so it's kind of wearing two hats. On the one hand you're providing crisis intervention, you know, the support, information, and referrals, and then on the other hand you're part of that criminal justice process, and you're kind of guiding them through that. . . . We do the psychological first aid or emotional triage, whatever you want to call it, and then as the case progresses, we pass the baton to the victim witness specialists at the district attorney's office.
>
> . . . When the police officers get on scene, they'll make a quick assessment of what the situation is and then call for us, and then once the police officer does their initial investigation, getting the names and the information, then we'll go in and sit with that victim, we'll make an emotional assessment— do they need crisis intervention, do they need medical attention, whatever is required and then we'll go from there . . . it frees up the police officers so they can get back to their investigation, and the other side of that is if someone feels that there is somebody in their corner helping them, they tend to make better witnesses. They tend to be more cooperative with the criminal justice process.

The victim advocate explains that being emotionally responsive to victims will cause them to be more reliable witnesses when court proceedings ensue. This demonstrates how the performance of emotional labor at the point when the state first assists the citizen pays dividends at the far end of the interaction.

Court proceedings may occur months or years after the crime. The state can only prevail when it has reliable witnesses.

It Is Not Public Service Motivation

In addition to the invisibility of emotional labor, there is confusion between emotional labor and related research streams. This is especially true vis-à-vis public service motivation, leadership, and emotional intelligence. That which differentiates emotional labor from these other topics is that it is an attribute of a job, while public service motivation, leadership, and emotional intelligence are personal attributes of the worker. In other words, the job requires emotional labor. By contrast, the worker has no need to engage in this level of emotive responsiveness with other strangers during off-duty hours.

The study of public service motivation, a term that refers to an individual's intrinsic predisposition to respond to motives grounded primarily or uniquely in public institutions and organizations, is a popular area of inquiry in public administration (Perry & Wise, 1990, p. 368). Motivation to serve the public is well established (Alonso & Lewis 2001; Frederickson & Hart 1985; Gabris & Simo 1995; Naff & Crum 1999; Perry 1996, 1997; Perry & Wise 1990). Those who score high on surveys of public service motivation subscribe to the nobility of the objectives of public service (Blumberg 1981).

David Coursey and Sanjay Pandey (2007) developed a scale to measure public service motivation that has three subdimensions: attraction to policy making, commitment to the public interest, and compassion. A sample item is "I unselfishly contribute to my community." One might think that this construct is linked to emotional labor. Hypothesizing that this was the case, Chih-Wei Hsieh (2009) employed the scale in a survey of midcareer public managers. Responses revealed the absence of a relationship between managers' scores on public service motivation and their ability to perform emotional labor. This led Hsieh to conclude that public service motivation and emotional labor, although seemingly related, are, in fact, two separate and distinct constructs. In retrospect, perhaps this is obvious: the former is attitudinal while the other is behavioral, unrelated to ideas of public service while directly related to emotive sensitivity.

The fundamental difference between the constructs of public service motivation and emotional labor is where each is "located." While the former is not anchored in a particular job and may not involve formal employment at all, the latter is specific to a job. Public service motivation is what drives a person to serve. It is not a required element of a public service job. One's inspiration to serve the public lies within oneself; it is neither an attribute of a job, nor a condition to obtain one.

It Is Not Leadership

Leadership is similarly conflated with emotional labor, but it is intertwined between the individual and the context of the job. The emotive component of leadership is an essential one, because it is "a series of social exchanges in which the leader can drive the other person's emotions into a better or worse state" (Goleman 2006, p. 276). Berman and West describe leadership as "relationship management [that] involves effective communication, teamwork, and conflict management skills, as well as the ability to help people work toward common objectives" (2008, p. 743). Leadership is a personal attribute exercised in a complementary context that suits the individual's style. Emotional labor, on other hand, is an element of the job. While emotional labor comes from the nature of the work, leadership, public service motivation, and emotional intelligence are qualities of the worker.

It Is Not Emotional Intelligence

Emotional labor is confused most often with emotional intelligence due to the similarity of the words, but the two differ considerably. Emotional intelligence is a broader term than emotional labor in that it denotes the individual's *capacity* to recognize emotions in self and other, much as cognitive intelligence measures the capacity to perform analytic and verbal tasks (Newman, Guy, & Mastracci 2009; Wong & Law 2002). It is emotional intelligence that makes it possible to recognize emotions in oneself and others and to use this knowledge for improved self-management and relationships with others (Goleman 2006). Some of the key skills characterizing emotional intelligence are active listening, acknowledging others, and mindful speaking (Berman & West 2008, p. 744). Emotional intelligence provides the substrate by which a worker has the ability to perform emotional labor. Again, the former is located in the person while the latter is located in the job. The latter is a noun: "She exerts emotional labor." The former is an adjective: "She is emotionally intelligent."

Berman and West acknowledge the difference between a personal characteristic and a job trait by noting the individual capacities to learn emotional labor skills: "People vary in their ability to learn these skills, a fact that may reflect personality or predispositions" (2008, p. 743). An emotionally intelligent person oftentimes works in a job that demands emotional labor skills (Carmeli 2003), but that need not be so. Indeed, an emotionally intelligent person need not be employed at all. She can be the good listener at a cocktail party or the good friend who always seems to know the right thing to say. By definition, however, an "emotional laborer" *must* be employed and must hold a job that demands emotional labor. Berman and West (2008, p. 743) demarcate this distinction as well: "Though not limited to the workplace, [emotional intelligence] is relevant to workplace settings." Emotional intelligence is required in the workplace when the job requires emotional labor. In fact, a substantial stream of research on emotional intelligence in psychology examines it outside the workplace altogether. Such studies include emotional intelligence and personal development (Izard 1992; Richards & Gross 1999; Wharton & Erickson 1995), and education (Mayer & Salovey 1993; Salovey & Mayer 1990). But studies of emotional labor are not done in the abstract. Rather, they must involve the workplace for that is where it occurs.

Another facet of emotional labor that sets it apart from emotional intelligence is the ability of the emotional laborer to switch it on and off. Those who work in jobs that require emotional labor can disengage at the ends of their shifts, and some *must* do so in order to cope with emotionally intense work. In fact, the personal relationships of those who perform emotionally intense jobs often suffer unless and until they learn how to let go of their workday experiences and separate their private lives from their work lives. The ability to deactivate their work personae at the end of the day is an important coping skill. When asked about the traits she seeks in job applicants, the executive director of a victim services agency identifies this ability as an important job skill:

> We're exposed to the roughest and the rawest experiences people can have and we see the meanest things that people do to each other so you've got to be in a place where you're able to do that work and then be able to go home and take care of yourself or be able to acknowledge that it's had an impact and be able to talk about the impact because it's human experience.

Elaborating on our earlier comparison between emotional and physical labor further illustrates the differences between emotional intelligence and emotional labor. Emotional intelligence is akin to physical fitness: The job that demands physical labor is parallel to one that demands emotional labor. To observe that someone is physically fit is to make a statement about the person, just as it is to say that someone is emotionally intelligent. The need to *exert* emotional labor is a characteristic of a job. Someone who is physically fit may or may not hold a job that requires physical labor, just as the emotionally intelligent person need not hold a job at all. Someone lacking physical fitness, however, would perform poorly at a job involving physical labor, just as one lacking emotional intelligence would perform poorly at a job that demands emotional labor. Likewise, a cognitively proficient person need not hold a job that demands cognitive skills—or hold a job at all. But the person wanting in cognitive ability would not perform well at a job requiring it.

Identifying unqualified job applicants, though, is far easier in physically and cognitively demanding jobs than it is in those requiring extensive emotional labor. Furthermore, it is interesting to note that the notion of "underemployment"—the employment of workers with high skill levels in low-skill and unskilled jobs—applies to the case when a cognitively adept person is employed in a job that does not call for high levels of cognitive skills. Not until emotional labor is elevated to its rightful status as a complex coordination of skills and behaviors will underemployment extend to instances when an emotionally intelligent person holds a job that does not demand those skills.

Emotional Labor: What It *Is*

Having carved out the negative space surrounding emotional labor, we now fill in its center:

> [Emotional labor] includes analysis and decision making in terms of the *expression* of emotion, whether actually felt or not, as well as its opposite: the *suppression* of emotions that are felt but not expressed. More specifically, emotional labor comes into play during communication between worker and citizen and it requires the rapid-fire execution of:
>
> - Emotive sensing, which means detecting the affective state of the other and using that information to array one's own alternatives in terms of how to respond
> - Analyzing one's own affective state and comparing it to that of the other
> - Judging how alternative responses will affect the other, then selecting the best alternative
> - Behaving, such that the worker suppresses or expresses an emotion—in order to elicit a desired response from the other. (Newman et al. 2009, p. 8, emphases supplied)

Service exchanges between worker and citizen require the worker to sense the right tone and medium for expressing a point and/or feeling and then to determine whether, when, and how to act on that analysis. To ignore this combination of analysis, affect, judgment, and communication is to ignore the social lubrication that enables rapport, elicits desired responses, and ensures that interpersonal transactions are constructive. It is an invisible but necessary element in person-to-person transactions. The emotional laborer must use her entire self as instrument to effect the transaction or behavior with the citizen. As one supervisor of victim advocates says, "They are the agent of change in that room. They are the tool so they have to bring all of themselves."

Emotional labor is the *effort within* oneself to conjure appropriate feelings or subdue inappropriate ones, and the effort to induce particular feelings in another person or stifle other feelings. "Appropriate" and "inappropriate" are defined by the job: If the worker cannot get the other person to feel and thus make a certain choice, then the job is not successfully executed. Repeated failures to do so will define the employee as someone who cannot do her job. But without "seeing" it, the problem will not be identified as related to emotional labor.

In sum, emotional labor is a skill that can be learned and refined. Its absence is manifested in substandard job performance and its presence by exceptional service. To reward or penalize workers for job outcomes without understanding the puppeteer within is to miss the opportunity to hire, train, and retrain public servants to their greatest potential. To concentrate on the marionette's arms and legs and not the hands above is to overlook the true locus of skill and ignore the interaction required to produce the service outcome.

How Emotional Labor Is Performed

In the excerpts that follow, each of the elements is present in the workers' descriptions of how they perform their jobs. Emotive sensing occurs at the outset as workers size up the emotional state of the citizen in need. Workers then take stock of their own emotional state in order to make sure that the emotion they are expressing is appropriate to their roles. Almost simultaneously, they have to determine how to act in order to elicit the desired response from the citizen as well as from coworkers. And finally, the workers must act. Below are the words of the workers as they describe this progression.

Psychological First Aid

This excerpt amplifies emotional labor in describing how the work of victim advocates is performed:

> Our most common callout is domestic violence . . . the first thing I'm going to do is introduce myself to that person, let them know what my role is because as a law enforcement–based advocate, I don't have confidentiality. I want to make sure that whoever I'm working with knows that so that they don't

tell me something I've got to then report to somebody else. So that pretty much comes out up front, and then I'll do that emotional assessment and do some crisis intervention. Everybody that's a victim advocate is trained in—well—I like the [term] "psychological first aid" better than "crisis intervention." The psychological first aid piece—we'll work with them, get them breathing, see if we can do a little bit of something to decrease those chemicals from being dumped, the cortisol and the adrenalin.

Interviewer: So you just sense where they are with that?

Yeah, and then try to bring that level down a bit. We go through a process. The first step is that we want them to feel safe and secure. We want to allow them to vent, whatever it is they have to vent, and we want to validate what they're feeling, and then we also want to prepare them for some things that they might experience over the next days and weeks and whatnot, and that's really a very short and dirty version of what crisis intervention or emotional triage is about. That can take anywhere from twenty minutes to an hour and a half to do that with somebody, depending on how traumatized they are, and how open they are in talking about what they're feeling. So once we get through that, the next thing that crime victims are desperate for is information. "I want to know what's going to happen next. Will you arrest my husband? Where is he going? Can I bond him out? When will he go to court or how do I keep him away from me? I'm scared." So we want to make sure they have a lot of information—and then we also want to do a needs assessment. What do you need now? Did they just take him to jail with the rent money in his pocket? How do we get that? How do we get the keys to your car? How do you get a protection order? We want to do a needs assessment. What do you need to get through the next couple of days, weeks? I don't want to give them too much because, really, when they're in that heightened emotional state you don't want to give them more than they can handle and they're not going to remember it. So we try to either write things down or give them one day at a time. Let's just deal with what do you have to do tomorrow, and not two weeks from now or three months from now.

Compartments and Closets

Emotional labor involves expression as well as suppression. The latter occurs, for example, when a worker has witnessed a horrific incident and has to "put it away" in order to be able to function. A firefighter referred to this as putting intense images in "little closets in my mind" and described the type of event that he keeps in one of those "little closets":

> We had a fire on Thanksgiving and the house had burglar bars all the way around. You know, the iron bars all the way around and a fully involved house fire where you pull up and there's flames coming out of every window and we didn't know if there was anyone in there or not. I forced the door and the hose crew started to go in and there was a person—we couldn't even see him he was burned so bad. There was a person lying right by the door, who was locked in—we ended up finding the key at the opposite end of the house. He tried to escape—the key was on the opposite end of the house and he burned to death right there and we didn't even see him. The first guy that went in stepped on him, he was burned so bad.

This excerpt demonstrates the detail with which the firefighter recalls the scene. Wrapped in emotion, the incident is seared in his memory. In order to respond to the next fire and the next and the next, the firefighter puts this recollection in a "little closet," only peeking at it occasionally. Importantly, experimental psychologists have observed that the need to focus on an objective task—intubating a patient, coordinating firefighters on the scene—actually facilitates the process of emotion suppression through compartmentalization. In other words, rigorous training on standard operating procedures and the need to focus on a specific task at hand can distract crisis responders from the highly intense emotionality of the incident. "Performing the working memory task may actually have operated as an emotion-regulation strategy itself, making it easier for participants to distract themselves from their [emotionally charged] memories" (Scheibe & Blanchard-Fields 2009, p. 221).

One's ability to compartmentalize work experiences is related to setting aside one's own feelings so that emotionally intense incidents do not infect the rest of the workday. Here a nurse who examines sexual assault victims and collects physical evidence for later legal proceedings describes how her work is performed. She explains that each person she works with is unique:

> The range of patients that we see is all over the place and none of them are going to be exactly alike, so that's important to go into it knowing you're not necessarily going to be able to go out in the waiting area and say, oh, that must be my patient because she looks a certain way. And, you know, you can't do this kind of work, which really shows you the darker side of our society in a lot of ways, and not have some kind of resiliency in yourself because just day in and day out we are exposed to this kind of violence.
>
> *Interviewer: When you feel that resiliency weakening, what do you do?*
>
> Well, I personally take a step back and go back to why am I doing this and it's being able to make that impact on someone's life who's just gone

through this terrible event. That is why I'm doing it. Fortunately for me, I can pretty easily compartmentalize things in my brain so that one really bad experience that I saw or, you know, the three in a row that I did, I can tuck that away in one place; not have it leak out into everything else in life. I think for anyone to be successful in this work they have to be able to do that because to go through, you know, what we see and let it impact every aspect of your life you can't—I don't think you can survive and keep doing the work.

Crazy Calm

Simultaneous suppression of one feeling while expressing another is a complex type of emotional labor that requires focused concentration. In the vignette below, the leader of an emergency response team, knowing that emotional states are contagious, sets the pace for how teammates respond to the chaos of an emergency situation. "Crazy calm" is how the captain in a large city fire rescue department describes his emotional control when on a call. He uses this technique to keep himself calm and keep everyone on the team focused and confident:

The hardest part is not getting excited before you get there, staying calm so that you can have a level-headed approach and keep everyone safe, which is really my main concern . . . a lot of times I'm talking to myself in my head. I really think about my breathing a lot. It's really noisy, you know. The sirens, the horns, going through traffic, and if I start breathing fast, it affects everything else, so it doesn't sound like a lot but you're putting on your bunker gear and you get your jacket on and you stop for a second and you go, wow, I'm breathing really quickly. And I'll stop what I'm doing even if it's only for two or three seconds and I'll take a big deep breath and I'll go okay, collect yourself, because not only that, I'm expected to talk when I get there. Let's say I'm first and I have to get on the radio and size up the scene for all the other incoming units, and if I'm breathing fast or if I sound excited and nervous I've noticed it has a domino effect. If I'm calm, everyone stays calm. If I'm nervous and excited, scared, if I project those things, then it really affects everyone. It doesn't even have to be an emergency. It could be somebody complaining of chest pain, and if I get excited because they can't get an IV [going] or they're having difficulties, it always goes badly after that. . . .

Once you start slowing down your voice, all that hysteria just starts to really slow down. It almost goes away. I mean people can be dying and the hysteria will go away because you learn to calm down, you slow everything down, you go . . . "I want you to do this and this." . . . It's kind of like leading the flock, you know what I mean? And once you go and you do that, everybody seems to gather around you. [And I control] my facial expressions. I'm very expressive, so if I look at them and go "hey, do I look nervous?" When I get nervous, you get nervous. And usually that works 90 percent of the time. People just calm right down. And on the radio the same thing—when I'm on the radio and I'll give commands or ordering new units or other things or tactics or whatever, nice and calm on the radio, those things will get accomplished. It's very commanding. People think that if you yell and you scream, you'll get things done, but it's the opposite.

Interviewer: From having a perspective of calm, is that something that you sort of wear or put on? You know, acting?

It all depends on the situation. More often than not, I've had experience in it to where it is who I am. I'm pretty calm. I know what the outcome is, and I know it's really not that bad. Other times I would say, ten percent of the time when we have something really good, I could be racing as fast as they are but since I conditioned myself to this thing and it becomes a condition, I can recognize it and feel that anxiety building within me and realize that I still need to maintain that crazy calm command person that I have—even though I could be going crazy inside. I feel it. And you feel the anxiety and you feel everything else but you know it works for you. . . . I'm as nervous as the guys are, but I don't believe that they see it.

Interviewer: So you purposefully work to mask that nervousness?

Absolutely.

Interviewer: In order to get the job done?

In order to provide the leadership role and to [control] the demeanor of the whole group in order to get that job done.

The use of "crazy calmness" is a technique that requires the worker to suppress, or turn, his own emotional state into an opposite state in order to execute the job. It is a skill that is expected for first responders. Those who fail at it are ostracized by their teammates. A variant of this type of emotional labor occurs when workers put their emotions on hold, as described below.

Workers often have to suppress their own emotion and, in its place, express a different emotion. The ability to suppress one's own feeling while exhibiting another requires focus, and those who are called upon to do so describe their emotional state as if pressing a pause button. An emergency medical technician (EMT) describes a call that required the team to extricate a badly injured child from a car:

> You kind of go into autopilot and like, for instance, on that call itself there really weren't any emotions that I noticed. It's not until afterwards when you stop acting that you start reflecting on what happened. Then you start to feel those kinds of things. . . . I think the people that do well in this field are the ones that automatically separate the emotion while you're working, but then the problem is, some people are better able to cope with that outside work when the call is over and some people aren't. I'm lucky . . . and then like I said at the station, depending on your crew, some people can sit down and talk about it and sometimes you can't, so, on the call itself, I think most people just block out that emotion automatically and it's not until you stop working that you realize that it's there and then you start thinking about it.

As metaphors, compartments and closets can be seen as attempts to dehumanize the self in order to take control over highly charged emotional situations. Compartments and closets are inanimate—they have no feelings—so envisioning oneself as comprised of "little closets in my mind" can be a way to deal with a crisis incident while not getting personally involved. Humor can be placed on the other end of the spectrum: using one's humanity, one's emotions, to deal with emotion-laden circumstances.

Humor

A sexual assault nurse examiner employs spontaneous decision making to assess the victim's state of mind in order to respond in a way that elicits a constructive response. The supervisor of sexual assault nurse examiners explains how nurses often use humor to relax victims:

> So many of my nurses will say "I try to use humor if I can when talking with my patients to help them relax and, you know, smile and laugh a little bit." The approach is always going to be different.

Humor is also a way for workers to cope with horrific situations when the mind can hardly comprehend what the eyes are seeing. Here an EMT gives an example:

> Person committed suicide—walked in front of a train and was severely dismembered so our job is to go pick up parts and clean it up and the train is still sitting there. It's not the easiest process to get around and I had an

arm without a hand attached and I said, hey, give me a hand, would you? And I handed it to him—a teammate—and believe it or not, he left. He left that night and he left the department. I kind of felt bad; I mean sometimes joking is a way to get through these kinds of events.

Common Sense

What does it take to do this sort of work? The captain of a fire-rescue unit says, "I've always thought that the best firemen are not the smartest firemen, not the most intelligent, but the firemen who have the greatest sense of common sense." This common sense, he explains, is the ability of firefighters to size up a situation quickly, determine how to resolve it while keeping everyone safe, and to put the plan in motion, all the while maintaining control over their emotions. A firefighter says that maintaining his self control is the way he manages to perform on the job:

> The time when I get the most mad at myself is when I've lost control. When they've seen me lose control. You can ask my wife. I'll go home and be pissed for a day. They saw me get mad. For me, when you walk in a fire with me or when you walk into a traumatic call with me, I want everyone to feel like wow, the captain knows what he's doing and he's calm. The biggest compliment they tell me is "You were a cool cat on that scene." . . . and inside I might have been suppressing it, but I know that I projected confidence, calm, confident approach which again affects them.

A firefighter says, "As a firefighter you know you're that hope for that person who called 911 and if you don't have it together, if you're not able to stay focused then that hope has just been washed away." All these processes combine to become what we call emotional labor. Its performance requires skill and energy and a successful outcome for the intervention depends on it. As brutal as many of the incidents are and as lingering as their memories of the horrors they witness are, those who perform the work report high levels of job satisfaction.

The Upside of Emotional Labor

For all the rigors of the work, the rewards are even greater. An EMT explains how his work motivates him:

> When you save people's lives and you make a difference, it's the most amazing thing. I worked on a guy—a cardiac arrest—was in the attic—

twenty-five years old—electrocuted—pulled him out of the attic. I worked this guy on the ground for over an hour on scene. CPR over an hour. He'd come back, he'd go away, he'd come back, he'd go away, come back and go away. I didn't give up—I was his best shot. Got a pulse back, got his heart rate back, brought him to the hospital, neurologist on the scene said "nice job, guys" . . . three months later I show up in the emergency room, nurse says, hey, you know that kid you worked on? He's out of the hospital. He's walking around. All he has is short-term memory loss. He still has the burn marks from the times we defibrillated him. I walked in—the mother and the sister recognized me. Hugged me, kissed me, bawling their eyes off that I saved her brother and her son's life—because I diligently worked that guy for an hour. I did not quit. I did not. That's what keeps you going. That's what's amazing—that—nobody else saved that guy. It was me. I was in charge of that scene. I didn't give up on him. I didn't want to run. I did it. That keeps me going because you know it'll happen again. You know you'll save somebody else's life and give them an opportunity. We only have one shot in this world. I gave that guy two. That's an amazing feeling, you know? If that doesn't keep you going, what would? That's why we're in it. That's what we do.

He explains further: "the passion and the desire that I have to help people basically, you know, is the fuel for my get-up-and-go, my urge to want to continue to do what I do and help people." In a similar vein, a member of an urban search and rescue team assigned to rescue operations following the disastrous Haitian earthquake of 2010 tells how it feels to search for survivors:

We didn't know exactly where this girl was and it was getting late at night. We drilled a hole [through multiple slabs of concrete] and they take a camera in and put it through and we had one of our chiefs who was an interpreter speaking to her and it was interesting. He said to go toward [the light]. She's been in there four days. So he said try to move towards the light where the camera went to the hole and the light and we're looking at it and suddenly her hand just pops up in front of the camera . . . it's one of those things we'll never forget. Because we have simulators, we have manikins, we have the whole thing, but you're watching it in the camera and it's just rubble and then someone's hand comes in front of it and starts shaking. It's one of those moments you'll never forget.

Examples such as the earthquake rescue and the EMT's success story demonstrate that great emotional intensity can result in great reward. But these rewards come at a cost. Next we discuss the deleterious effects of this work.

The Downside of Emotional Labor

Despite the high job satisfaction that emotional labor brings, there is a down-side that makes the work risky. Those who engage in emotional labor are vulnerable to burnout. Intense exposure to protracted emotional stress can result in post-traumatic stress as well as vicarious trauma. Both of these result in diminished effectiveness on the job. Those who manage agencies where emotional labor is essential for job performance are wise to take steps to miti-gate this risk. The coordinator of the sexual assault nurse examiner (SANE) program in a large metropolitan area describes the importance of being able to cope with the job. She says that for anyone to be successful in this type of work they have to be able to tuck away their experiences and not have them "leak out" into the other parts of their lives. She said that, otherwise, workers could not keep doing their jobs.

Vicarious trauma is the term for the emotional toll of experiencing hor-rific events secondhand. The impact of the situation still affects workers even though they are not victims. Burnout may occur from performing emotionally-intense work without dealing with the vicarious trauma that accompanies it. Says a victim services coordinator,

> It's after a while when you start to forget, "Yeah, I'm fine. Oh, I've done a million of these, you know?" And I always tell people, when you say I can do a domestic violence call with my eyes closed, you better get out and do something else.

Emotionally intense work is energy consuming in and of itself. When it occurs in crisis situations where workers may, or may not, save a life, it is even more all-consuming. When extraordinary effort produces success, the personal rewards are considerable. But when efforts do not succeed, the outcome extracts a toll. An important survival skill is for workers to make peace with the fact that they cannot always be successful. Dealing with the futility of other people's situations—and the futility of their work efforts—requires a way of thinking that frees the worker from self-blame. One of the drawbacks to working with victims of domestic violence is the possibility that the victim will be hunted by the abuser and killed. A director of counseling and advocacy services for victims of domestic abuse explains how she dealt with the murder of a client:

> I have to know that I really have no power to keep her safe. I don't. I can give her ideas, I can give her suggestions, I can talk to her about options, I can talk to her about my fears for her, I can talk to her about what I see

is dangerous behavior, high-risk behavior, I can help her to be able to assess that better, or more consciously, because actually she's probably been assessing it pretty well because she's still here. But she's been doing it subconsciously, if you will, and so I want to help her become conscious about that assessment in order to be able to more quickly protect herself and her kids. But I can't keep her safe. There's nothing I could do. If someone wants to kill her, there's a good chance that's going to happen, and there's nothing I can do about that. I can do everything I can in that moment that I'm with her to avoid that, or to prolong that, but I can't stop it. And I have to be able to accept that to do this work . . . I must not think I'm anything more than just a woman who's perhaps seen more cruelty in relationships than your general person does and that I think about it more than the general population does. But that's all I am. I can't stop anything, and I have to know that.

Analogous to the reality of domestic violence work is what emergency rescue squads label a "bad call." For those who work in emergency rescue, success means that the victim is safely rescued and all teammates are uninjured in the process. Failure in that effort is defined as a bad call. Coping with that failure is described this way by a member of an air rescue helicopter team:

Just understanding that there's nothing that I could have done more than what I did. I think a lot of the times we assist in anything that we can depending on what we're called on, but I think in reality when something like that bothers you, in myself I like the quiet place, and I like to think back on my own and say well, you know, I didn't cause that individual to get into that accident. We didn't cause that individual to lose himself in the Everglades or go into deep water where he drowned, or hang himself. . . . I didn't put that person in harm's way. I was there to assist.

How the Parts Fit Together

How, precisely, does emotional labor relate to job satisfaction and burnout? From prior research (Hsieh, Jin, & Guy, 2011), we know that it has a positive, direct effect on job satisfaction. The more that emotional labor is performed, the higher is the worker's level of job satisfaction. We also know that those who perform emotional labor have high levels of personal efficacy, which means that they are able to identify when emotion work is necessary and they are able to manage their own emotions as well as the emotions of others in order to engage in it. Workers who are efficacious—capable of managing their emotions while also managing the emotional state of others—score high in terms of their level of job satisfaction and score low in terms of burnout.

Figure 2.1   **Emotion Work's Relationship to Personal Efficacy, False-Face Acting, Job Satisfaction, and Burnout**

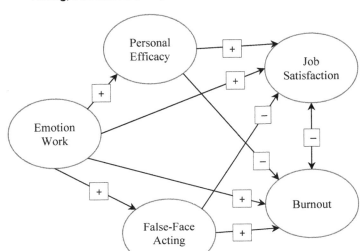

Note: Each valence in the illustration represents a statistically significant relationship at the p < .05 level.

We also know that those who identify the need for emotion work and who perform it are also skilled in false-face acting. This term refers to workers' ability to suppress their own emotion while exhibiting an opposite feeling. In other words, they can wear a mask, a false face, acting one way while actually feeling another way. The downside of their ability to pretend to feel one way when actually feeling another is that this sort of emotional labor results in high levels of burnout and low levels of job satisfaction. In fact, when burnout happens, false-face acting takes the form of pretending to care when actually feeling dead inside.

Employers describe burnout as "heart death" for workers engaged in emotional labor. In the field, workers refer to burnout as getting "crispy." They become more mechanical in their discussions with coworkers. They start blaming the victim or referring to cases as if each accident is an unfortunate but emotively sterile event. Burnout is inversely related to job satisfaction. Figure 2.1 illustrates these interrelationships.

Hsieh, Jin, and Guy (2011) surveyed workers in a wide range of public service jobs in order to come to these conclusions. Survey respondents represented a mix of jobs, including human service providers in social service settings, attorneys, detectives, social workers, prison officials, 911 call takers, and workers who receive citizen complaints about faulty consumer products. In other words, some were first responders who interacted with citizens for only a few minutes and received no feedback about the results of their actions. Some were professionals who worked with the same client for years. And some were clerical staff whose work was fairly routine and in which they learned the outcome of every case they dealt with. The common thread of these varied jobs was that each required the worker to be in direct communication with a citizen, providing a service that was unique to public service. Citizen met state in each interaction. And regardless of the nature of the interaction, the dynamics of emotional labor were similar.

Summary

The theory of emotional labor and the practice of emotional labor coincide. While theory presents the process, workers' words explain what it feels like. Their stories tell the distinct steps and processes that they use when performing it. The worker is engaged from the initial sizing up of the situation to determining which emotion should be elicited from the citizen and which emotion should be displayed to achieve that response. And the performance continues almost like a play, with workers doing whatever it takes to ensure that the necessary emotion is displayed. If this means suppressing an opposite emotion, then that is what the worker must do. If it means displaying an emotion that one does not intrinsically feel, then that must be done. The upshot is that the outcome of the exchange between worker and citizen depends on the performance of emotional labor.

The work of first responders is emotionally intense, so they must find a way to deal with the mental and emotional images that stay with them long after the crisis has been resolved. Workers use a variety of strategies to deal with these recollections that become seared in their minds. Whether they use "little closets" in their minds to sequester intense memories, whether they adopt a "crazy calm" countenance as they approach a hair-raising scene, or whether they push their "pause button," responders figure out a modus operandi that works for them. Even humor has a role in emotionally intense situations, as it disarms tension.

Emotional labor is different from public service motivation in that the latter refers to a worker's interest in advancing the welfare of the community. The former refers to work performance that involves emotive tasks. In theory, those with higher levels of emotional intelligence are more capable of performing the work than those who have lower levels.

In some ways, the vernacular term "street smarts" captures this dynamic in that the worker reads the emotive state of the citizens involved and accommodates to it in order to effectuate a transaction. If citizens need to be calmer, the worker must calm them. If citizens are angry, the worker must resolve their anger. If citizens are panicked, the worker must calm them and help them gain control. If citizens are belligerent, the worker must engage them in such a way that they agree to comply. The "scientific" approach to management ignores this emotive aspect of job performance. Instead, it focuses on cognitive aspects of the job, prescribing processes and procedures that standardize interactions with citizens. Emotional labor, on the other hand, is, by its very commission, spontaneous and unique to each situation and each citizen's interaction with the state. It is very real and it is not programmable. The director of a shelter for victims of domestic violence says,

> We're constantly reevaluating how situations are going because you can't ever predict. I mean, we can have all these policies and procedures about how you handle situations and then next week one will pop up that's not like any of the others and we won't know how to handle it. We talk a lot about our top guiding principles: we want to make sure everybody's safe; we want to make sure that their stay is kept confidential; we want to make sure that we're obeying the law. We want to make sure of these top things and if we're doing that in every decision and every situation, then we're most likely doing the right thing. . . . [In each case], everything is going to be different, so using these kind of guidelines, then we're probably on the right track.

This quote shows how workers are trained to use their own discretion while using guiding principles as their boundaries in unique situations. In the words of those who perform it, emotional labor gives meaning to workers' lives. A firefighter describes what retirement feels like:

> After you retire you think you're not gonna miss it and there's not a day that goes by that you don't—you know everybody needs to be needed. Some people just need to help.

The firefighter's words capture the rewards of emotion work. As demanding as it is, responding emotionally to intense situations provides engagement and immediate feedback. For workers who perform such work, the absence of emotionally charged interactions leaves them wanting.

3

Human Capital Issues

The work of first responders is labor intense. It cannot be performed by a machine. So human resource issues are important, from recruiting to hiring to training to retaining. The Denver Center for Crime Victims maintains a hotline for calls from anyone who has been victimized by a crime. Cathy Phelps (2010), its executive director, uses this mantra with her staff: "If you can't take care of yourself, you can't take care of the victim." She emphasizes that the work of listening professionals takes a toll. To prevent this from affecting performance, she requires all staff to implement and follow a self-care plan that they update annually. She says it is amazing what people get done in a year and how great they feel about it. She credits the plan for lower absenteeism, lower worker compensation claims, better morale, and longer tenure with the agency.

Employers' assumptions about emotional labor influence how they expect employees to handle its effects. These assumptions are influenced by two understandings: dispositional and dramaturgical. The dispositional perspective assumes that emotions arise based on uniquely individual characteristics, wholly unrelated to organizational control. This leads to a focus on individual differences as they pertain to emotive expression, self-efficacy, and emotional intelligence (Liu, Perrewe, Hochwarter, & Kacmar 2004; Opengart 2005; Schaubroeck & Jones 2000). On the other hand, the dramaturgical view is that emotions arise on the basis of social interaction. This approach assumes that they are subject to organizational control, which in turn leads to a focus on organizationally mandated display rules (e.g., Ashforth and Humphrey 1993; Ekman 1973; Hochschild 1979, 1983). Both of these approaches are partially correct. There can be mutual influences between organizational rules and personal traits that determine workers' emotional coping strategies. These influences include antecedents, correlates, and consequences of emotive behavior.

"What-to-do" display rules, meaning mandates to express or suppress particular types of emotions, cause the clerks at drive-up hamburger shops to wear a smile and close the transaction with a friendly wish to "have a nice day." "What-not-to-do" rules result in hiding or faking felt emotions. For example, emergency medical responders will not express horror when seeing a victim's wounds. A law enforcement officer told us that "crying is not an option when you're trying to deal with someone who is crying about a loved one dying." As earlier vignettes demonstrate, emotional labor often requires workers to suppress the emotion they are experiencing and to display a different emotion. We call this *false-face acting*. It is as important to job performance as authentic expressions of emotion are. Such emotion regulation is risky for workers, however, because, if not managed, it is likely to result in burnout.

Strategies for Dealing with the Downside

There are strategies employers can use to mitigate the risks of emotional labor. The three methods that are used most commonly are formalized critical incident stress management, which usually relies on critical incident debriefings; self-care plans; and recruitment processes that emphasize the importance of the job applicant's being self-aware.

Critical Incident Stress Management

"Critical incident stress management" is the term used by law enforcement, firefighters, and emergency rescue squads for combating the harmful effects of emotionally intense work. The procedure most frequently used is *critical incident debriefings*. These are meetings attended by a counselor and the team members who were involved together in an emotionally intense situation. They discuss the event and everyone's feelings about it in a manner that suits the workplace culture. The debriefings may be required or voluntary. The goal is to resolve lingering images, reactions, and memories. The debriefings serve a valuable function in dealing with vicarious trauma and post-traumatic stress by helping workers deal with intense emotions they had to suppress while the encounter was ongoing. A firefighter describes a debriefing this way:

> When you get to sit in that room with those people and everybody's honest, if you have the right personalities that take it seriously, you come to realize how everybody felt that same frustration and that you, no matter what you did, you wouldn't have been able to change the outcome at that point because obviously it's internalized.

Another firefighter describes his experience with debriefings:

> And then there is critical stress debriefing—personnel that we have come up to the fire stations and they talk about it and anytime we have any type of situations like that we do sit down and we talk with them and they say okay—how are you feeling? I know I've had to do it one or two times but I've also learned how to deal with it. . . . Could we have done better? Could we have gone in this window instead of this door to get to that child? So, you know, you try your best to adapt—you try your best to find that avenue of peace where you're able to say okay, you know what? I've done all that I was capable of doing.

In this case, operational issues were discussed during the debriefing, although operational judgments are supposed to be reserved for separate sessions devoted to technical and procedural issues. Critical stress debriefings are designed explicitly to focus on the feelings that were aroused by the call. They are, however, only effective when those attending are responsive and resist the temptation to focus on topics that are easier to discuss, such as equipment and procedures. It is also important that discussions during the debriefing get left at the door as responders exit the meeting. For the debriefing to be effective, however, responders often need to revisit the discussion later and process its nuances. For instance, a detective told us, "The problem is that the officers can go in there and choose not to participate or participate minimally and so it doesn't get addressed; then it's just a box that is ticked off." As an example, the detective explained that she supervised an officer who was involved in a shooting in which he severely injured the person who was trying to run over him. This was a "good shoot" by the department's standards:

> But there wasn't the kind of care for this man's psyche on how it would actually affect him. So for two years he's under various supervisors over here, and there are complaints from other officers about how he's angry, he's not effective, he's not handling his cases very well—for two years! And then I'm transferred over here and he's now one of my officers that I have to supervise, and I immediately do an evaluation that's not a nice evaluation. It says you need to look at this, you need to take care of this, and so forth. I talk to him and within a week, he has a breakdown and breakthrough and we end up sending him to a trauma center to look at the issues that came up in the shooting that nobody ever, ever dealt with him before. I think he's on the road to recovery, but that's two years for post-traumatic stress to sit in the back of his brain creating damage, but we as a [police] culture don't want to look at that yet.

These words amplify a quandary. Police and firefighter culture is known to discourage expression of emotions that are other than tough and self-confident.

Officers are reluctant to express doubts, fears, or regrets because they fear ostracism by their peers. And to disclose personal misgivings is to alert teammates to weakness, which they may fear will jeopardize their safety on the next bad call. While expressions of empathy are acceptable, expressions of loss of control are not. Critical incident debriefings are designed to overcome this block to an honest exchange of feelings, but sometimes they do not succeed.

Self-Care Plans

Another strategy that is effective in helping workers prevent burnout is a *self-care plan*. Used predominantly among victim assistance workers and domestic violence workers, a self-care plan can be required by the employer. Its purpose is to preemptively keep responders healthy. It involves the employees' specifying personal goals for themselves on an annual basis. The goals may or may not be work-related and always relate to personal growth. The ultimate purpose of the plan is to remind workers that their lives and personal growth are separate from the work they perform.

Cathy Phelps, executive director of the Denver Center for Crime Victims, is a strong advocate of self-care plans and insists that each employee have one. When workers have their annual performance appraisal, they are evaluated on their progress toward achieving goals in their self-care plan, just as they are evaluated on the various dimensions of their specific job. A plan includes stretch goals in the areas of physical, emotional, financial, intellectual, and/ or spiritual health. Within the first thirty days of employment, workers are required to create their plan and state it in measurable, outcome-oriented terms. Phelps (2010) explains, "We are the witness to horrible things that we have to be able to absorb and work with; you can't do that if you're not practicing self-care and if you don't have an environment that supports that practice."

As executive director of a nonprofit agency, Phelps chides sister agencies for waiting too long before insisting that employees take care of themselves:

> The nonprofit human services sector says we think self-care's important but at the point at which they encourage you to do it, you're already crisp. And a bubble bath is not going to do it. And a vacation is not going to do it. And a cup of herb tea is not going to do it. So we try to have something that is more sustainable and more self-directed.

To reiterate her commitment to requiring self-care plans, Phelps says, "I can walk into any number of nonprofits and see who is crisp (i.e., burned out)— you feel it walking in the door. They just don't have it anymore." About the success of self-care plans at her agency, Phelps says, "You know I just know how I used to feel and how I feel now and that I never have a day when I don't want to come to work and this is hard work so it must be working."

Emotional labor is performed in some venues that are not anticipated, and strategies are necessary for addressing work issues. Take the case of translators who work for victim assistance programs. For example, the Denver Center for Crime Victims has several translators on staff so that the center can respond to anyone who calls, regardless of the language they speak. When translating, interpreters speak in the voice of the crime victim: "We're the ones that are speaking in the first person—*I* was raped, *I* was—you know, and nobody's recognizing what that does to *us*." So the Denver Center developed a workshop for the translators, similar to the critical incident debriefings that police and firefighters have at their disposal.

Some domestic shelters have a less formalized system of self-care, involving extra vacation time on an as-needed basis. Here are words from a shelter director:

> Generally all of my staff have self-care plans that they lay out for themselves and they do it yearly . . . you give and you pour and you pour and you pour and sometimes you just need time away to fill yourself back up again.

In addition to self-care plans and critical incident debriefings, hobbies also help workers decompress, taking their attention away from work experiences and focusing their energy on something totally different. A female firefighter says,

> Hobbies, jokes, sometimes it can be a good cry. Exercise tends to help a lot, short term, but there's still a lot that just sometimes it's time [that helps] to get past it, and reassurance from other people that you did everything you could do.

Responders who succeed in preventing burnout learn to treat mistakes and bad calls as learning opportunities. They are able to talk about their experiences and feelings to someone whom they trust, whether it is a supervisor, teammates, or spouse. And all report a strong bond of trust among team members. Trust among coworkers, a willingness to talk about the experience and debrief, and a focus on learning from bad outcomes in order to improve performance the next time seem to combine to prevent burnout. In our interviews, employers also speculated on effective ways for workers to think about their experiences on the job. When we asked a police officer about the characteristics of those who are better at handling this kind of stress than others, she responded,

It has to do with folks that are able to understand that there's a larger plan. Now I'm not necessarily speaking about religion or necessarily spirituality, but the ones that tend to be horrified and can't get through it are the ones that can't understand the kind of trauma and violence that they encounter, so they get stuck there. The ones that can say things like "I know that I'm a tool for God" or "I understand that this may be a larger plan and this is just my job or my function," they have a concept of who they are in the game, so to speak. And again, I really am not referring to necessarily spirituality but to a larger picture of what they're doing, so that they don't get stuck in the mire of, you know, what is this all about? And here we go again. And the world is bad and we're just going downhill, rather than understanding that, you know, this is their job and their function and the next day is better and they may have another crisis but, you know, there's something beyond what they're doing.

One police officer says that workers who hold onto some sort of larger "value and meaning or align with some kind of sacredness" seem to do better in avoiding burnout. In contrast,

I've had two interviews where it was so apparent that the person was spiritually bankrupt. There was nothing left for them, and I didn't understand how they could even hold on. How do we help this person, you know? And that person had been in law enforcement for ten years but I know is not destined to remain much longer.

Elaborating, she explains the police culture and why dealing with traumatic experiences is difficult:

I think we have a lot [who] don't know why they survive, but they do, and a lot of that has to do with their ability to make some sense out of the meaninglessness of whatever they encounter. And I also think that the unfortunate thing is that this culture's not really ready to share, so they can't articulate it yet—not with themselves or others outside the culture. And in my opinion this culture is so amazing and has the potential to teach this to others that are coming into contact with trauma, whether it's just the average citizen or whoever as far as finding some resiliency and meaning. But we're going to have to get more open with who we are and what we are and recognize that there are limits in our abilities within the trauma and crisis. . . . We're all human beings and so we all pretty much respond pretty similarly. We just have been given this power and authority by the public and so that kind of jacks with our perception sometimes and makes us close down or hold that much closer to the vest than we need to.

Traits to Look For When Hiring Emotional Laborers

It is abundantly clear that, in addition to the work skills outlined in the job description, those who work in the front lines of public service must also have emotive skills. The traits required for successfully working in an emotionally intense, chaotic environment are elusive. Across the board, however, employers seek job applicants who are aware of their own reactions to trauma and are cognizant of the need to deal openly with the emotional intensity of their experiences. The director of a victim assistance program responded this way when we asked how she can tell whether a job applicant has the requisite level of self-awareness:

> If you can see that they've been successful in a field for a length of time, that's one good indication. . . . If I interview them I talk about previous victimization issues that they've ever had and what they did with that; I talk about self-care; I talk obviously about their experiences and their education and think about what they could bring to this organization. But primarily I'm looking for someone who is healthy and strong, someone who can work in a chaotic environment. . . . We might be working on a report and all of a sudden somebody calls and we have to go out on scene, and so we have to adjust to that a lot—someone who can think on their feet and has common sense, because I can train about victim issues, I can train about the system, but every single call is different, and then [an applicant must] be able to work as a self-directed person because this is not an environment where you punch in the clock.

When asked what she looks for in job applicants, the executive director of the Denver Center for Crime Victims says,

> I'm looking for self-awareness, self-management. We ask what strategies do you use to cope with stress and the answers are amazing. Some people think the answer is to tell us that they don't have any stress. That that's it. "Oh, I don't get stressed." Impossible. Others think, Wow! That's a good question. Let me think about it. . . . Self-awareness is huge. Self-management is huge. That's at the top of my list. You know, being able to know when you are out of sorts and out of order or your behavior is, and be interested in getting to the root of it and not, you know, blaming . . . that's hard for people, I think.

The director of a domestic violence center looks for similar traits when interviewing applicants who will provide services to residents in the shelter:

I think self-awareness is the biggest piece because you've got to be able to know what's going on for yourself and then either be able to step out of the situation or finish it up and then process that with a coworker or with your supervisor. I think that's huge.

The director of counseling and advocacy at a domestic violence shelter says that she also looks for self-aware job applicants:

As I'm assessing someone's ability to do this work, self-awareness is one of the first things I look for. How much do you know about you? What triggers you? I don't want to be your therapist. I don't want to hear about your past trauma. There are other places for you to do that. Your supervisor is not the place, but I need for you to be aware of those things in yourself and to not be afraid to face them, because it's your job to manage that.

A sexual assault nurse examiner talks about the traits she looks for when interviewing registered nurses for work as sexual assault examiners:

I look for people who verbalize, even without me asking, that they work with patients who experience trauma; you know, like an example would be labor and delivery nurses who specialize in fetal demise, like the mom [who] gives birth to a baby that has died. Obviously that's not a legal issue; it's not a forensic issue, but the trauma that that family experiences knowing that their baby has died is horrific. And to have nurses who tell me that that's what they want to take care of—that patient—then that gives me a pretty good clue that they can work well with patients who have experienced trauma. If I interview someone who talks about the forensic side of things in terms of, you know, "I've worked in the ER for twenty-five years and I've done probably twenty-five evidence collections as an ER nurse and I want to be involved in the legal system" and if they go through all of that and don't mention the patient, then they're not going to be a good fit for us because the patient care has to be at the top of the list. . . . Sometimes we see nurses who are CSI oriented, like "I think this is really cool and I want justice." We're very leery of those nurses, too, because honestly we don't see a lot of justice for our patients. We testify very little and that's because a lot of the time there is a plea bargain put in place, but as much of the time it's that the case just doesn't move forward because they can't put together a good case for a prosecution. So the justice part, even though that's the definition of why we're doing this, we don't see a lot of justice, so we make that very clear when we hear someone say "justice" and "I want to help get this guy" and "I want to be part of this criminal system and make a difference," then you're going to be really disappointed because we don't see that a lot.

Job applicants who respond that they do not experience stress are as unlike to be hired as those who admit to maladaptive behaviors such as drinking too much. As the above interviews suggests, self-awareness is paramount—an essential trait for hiring workers who must engage in emotionally-intense work. This trait enables workers to take stock of their own performance and to process their emotions.

Training and Supervision

The importance of training and supervision cannot be overemphasized. Ironically, most job descriptions fail to mention the emotional intensity of the work. For instance, those who respond to job ads for 911 call takers are often surprised to learn that in addition to being familiar with electronic dispatch systems, they must also be personally equipped to handle the emotional state of callers. It is this aspect of the work that sticks with them in the evening, long after they have removed the headphones and turned away from the dispatch console. The agencies that do the best job of training are those that focus on trauma and what victims of trauma experience as well as what workers may experience in the form of vicarious trauma. Here is how a victim services coordinator explains vicarious trauma:

> I live upstairs in a condo. So if I go grocery shopping and I have ten bags that I have to carry up the stairs I have two choices. I can make ten trips up and down the stairs and carry a bag each time. Or I can load those puppies up in my arms and make one hideous trip up the top of the stairs. Either way, I am going to be exhausted when I get done. Whether I run up and down ten times or whether I am carrying a heavy load once, the impact physically is going to be the same. I'm going to be exhausted. That's what it's like with vicarious trauma. You can either be called to a homicide where it's horrible and horrific and just raw emotion out there, or you can do five or six milder callouts in a row. In the end, you're going to be impacted on an emotional level. It's the same thing. So you want to be aware of that and have a heightened sense of self-awareness. How are you feeling? Are you cranky? Are you snapping at your kids and you're kicking the dog? Stop and think about, okay, what have I done? What am I reacting to here?

To help workers deal with the "multiple trips up stairs" as well as to help them with horrific events, this supervisor makes contact with the worker:

> I make sure I call everybody after a callout, no matter what it was. If it's a staff person, I sit down with them. If it's a volunteer, I call them on the phone: "Tell me what worked, what did you think went well with that call, what were the challenges, and tell me how you're feeling about this."

This approach attempts to help workers deal with the incident while it is fresh on their minds, as if debriefing after each flight of stairs.

Overcoming Emotion Overload

Another dimension to training workers who will be in emotionally-intense situations is to prepare them for managing their own emotional overload. A firefighter warns that, when approaching a burning building, you have to make sure it is safe to act: "It's very easy to get tunnel vision because of the adrenalin that's going on and it's like the moth to the fire and so that does take training to learn to get those parts of your emotions under control—the adrenalin-junkie emotions—because those are the ones that tend to get people seriously hurt." To further explain, she says,

> Perfect example—firefighters love to break things. I know it's a stereotype, but I don't know any firefighter that doesn't look forward to forcing entry. We were dispatched to assist police to force entry into an apartment. We arrived, myself and three other people, in the truck. Cops were there. They had an ex parte order that they were trying to serve. The person wouldn't open the door. They had gone and gotten a force order the day before. Now they're there to get in. They have the mother of the victim—the patient—and she had a key but it would only work on the top lock—didn't work—there was no lock on the doorknob but the doorknob was locked from the inside so they asked for our help. I asked the cops, any history of violence? No. Everybody was really relaxed and my guys had a sledgehammer in hand ready to just bang the door down. I said wait. Wait. Stop. Okay, guys, let's do this right. They had that emotion. They were ready to break things down. We stopped—we took the doorknob off. The door still didn't open. The crew was ready to break that door down and had I had that same emotional response on this call, somebody probably would be dead today because before my firefighter on the truck could start swinging the sledgehammer—he was a large guy, six-foot-four and over three hundred pounds so the door would have gone down—something, I don't know what—a guardian angel I call it—a sixth sense. For some reason I squatted down and looked through the hole we made where the doorknob used to be and this person was on the opposite side of the room with gun in hand aiming at the door. So that's where those emotions, that adrenalin—and that's not an instance that happens all the time—but you take a fire, people rush in without taking a look at the structure, what's going on with it, they can put themselves in a bad situation very quickly.

The supervisor for sexual assault nurse examiners describes her supervisory style:

Most of the time when we do have a pretty bad exam, usually that nurse reaches out either to me or to, you know, another friend that she has on the team to talk about it. If I happen to look at the photos, for instance, and see that there was a patient with a lot of trauma, and you know—the physical injury doesn't really compare to the emotional trauma—I mean, certainly, you can see a patient who doesn't have any physical sign but emotionally is a wreck and that's just as taxing as seeing the patient who has broken bones and, you know, bruising and bleeding. But I think, obviously, the physical injury can leave an impact in terms of just witnessing that and needing to photograph that and measure every injury and just have this really in-depth understanding of their physical presentation. So if I see things like that, you know, in looking at the photos or doing chart reviews, I'll contact that nurse and say, oh, this looked really bad, you know, are you okay or whatever.

Organizational culture dictates which emotions are appropriate to display and which ones are not. Whether norms are formally or informally expressed, they influence whether the worker disguises emotional expression or not. The police and firefighter culture is one of those with restrictive display rules, even when in conversation with each other. The secretive culture makes it difficult to discuss anxieties and shortcomings openly and deal with them constructively. Fields whose workforces are predominantly female, however, have an easier time addressing the emotive aspects of the job during training. As the quotes in this chapter demonstrate, those who work in predominantly female fields—domestic violence and victim assistance programs, for instance—address the emotive aspects of the job more openly than law enforcement or firefighters.

Staff Development

Efforts to help staff develop emotive skills and to cope with lingering reactions to intense situations must be culture-specific. In police and firefighter cultures, where expression of emotion is stilted at best, it is helpful to use words that do not connote signs of weakness and are not stigmatized as mental health "talk." The use of the term "critical incident stress management" provides a case in point. A generic term like "stress mitigation" also works in such a culture. But the message must be there, regardless of how it is wrapped: A readily available crib sheet that lists warning signs of post-traumatic stress can work if it is phrased in terms that tell how to identify warning signs in teammates rather than in oneself. This takes the onus off the worker reading the sheet. Warnings to watch for erratic behavior, excessive irritability, excessive drinking, and so forth, along with contact information for helpful resources, can be effective.

One of the important ways that self-awareness plays out for emotional laborers is that it helps them situate themselves, doing the type of work that is most rewarding. And this changes over the course of their careers. A counselor who works at a domestic violence shelter gives this explanation for why she started her career in direct services, then moved back and forth between administration and direct services:

> It's back to self-awareness. I think to do trauma work, one critical piece, if not the critical piece, is self-awareness and what's happening for me and how am I managing what I do. You know, how does it affect me? How do I balance? And finding the right place for yourself. . . . There are all different kinds of ways to do trauma work. There's all different kinds of ways to work with victims of crime, you know, and where am I best suited to do that? And I think it's also about ebb and flow. I've gone from management back to direct service and then back to management. That was good for me because that's part of my self-care, if you will. Because there's ups and downs to both things and so being self-aware and kind of knowing, okay, this is where I need to be now and making that transition and knowing that you can also transition back, you know, and if it's where you're supposed to be, I don't think it matters. To do this work is to pay attention to what you need and where you can be most effective right now for yourself and not worry about what that looks like anywhere else. I mean, I had people question me when I went back to direct service. Why did you do that? But that's just where I needed to be. I just needed that contact again, and it was good that I did it. It energized me.

Another aspect of developing workers occurs when a worker is promoted to an administrative position. A captain of a firefighting unit says it this way:

> I have to remember my role and the hardest thing any new officer will tell you is that: keeping the supervisory role—not putting down the clipboard and jumping in there because once you jump in there, then who's watching [out for everything]? You need somebody to supervise and it's a hard thing to do at first. I think it takes a little bit of time to develop that discipline and realize how important your role is even though you may not physically be working as hard as everybody else. You know mentally you are; maybe you're working harder mentally, but physically that's really a hard thing for firemen to do. To understand that, hey, my job has shifted from, you know, break this door down, put this fire out, to guide them there and make sure they're doing it safely. It's tough, you know?

Summary

Emotional labor is performed on the job and requires effort within the worker. Workers size up the emotional state of the citizen and then manage their own emotions as well as the emotions of the other. The purpose of this emotion management is to enable the task at hand in order to resolve the problem. Without it, the job cannot be successfully performed. While its performance leads to extraordinary job satisfaction, it also makes the worker vulnerable to burnout. Workers say that they love the work because they know they are making a difference in people's lives and that this makes emotional labor worthwhile. But for those who are unable to come to terms with how the work makes them feel, there is always the risk of post-traumatic stress disorder or vicarious trauma, both of which contribute to burnout.

Just as one would expect an employer to provide breaks from prolonged physical labor, there must also be accommodation to prolonged emotional labor. Staff development programs that are designed in such a way that they fit within the work culture and argot are more effective than programs that stigmatize workers who have turned "crispy."

This chapter reviewed two primary types of interventions: critical incident stress management, used most often in police and firefighter departments, and self-care plans, used most often in victim assistance and domestic violence work settings. Both rely on self-awareness as the vehicle for workers to come to grips with their experiences and their reactions to them.

There is also preemptive training that can forestall or prevent the downside to emotion work. Alerting workers that it is normal to experience intense, lingering images of horrific scenes helps them to understand that their reaction is predictable, rather than being a sign of weakness. All agree that responders must be well trained in the technical aspects of their jobs. But they must also be trained in the emotive aspects of their work.

4

Communicating Competence and Cultivating Trust

On August 23, 1992, Hurricane Andrew developed wind speeds reaching 175 miles per hour, becoming a Category 5 hurricane. It crossed the Bahamas, weakened slightly, then reenergized before making landfall and flattening Homestead, Florida. Both the east and west sides of the southern Florida peninsula had to prepare for storm surges and tornadoes even after the hurricane had passed. At the time, Hurricane Andrew was the costliest tropical storm in U.S. history, producing damage in excess of $41.6 billion in inflation-adjusted dollars (Pielke, Gratz, Landsea, Collins, Saunders, & Musulin, 2008); it is only second in devastation behind Hurricane Katrina. Both storms were so costly because they struck areas of population density; in fact, Hurricane Andrew was the first to have hit such densely populated areas. In Dade County alone, ninety percent of all homes had major roof damage, and in total, 117,000 homes were destroyed or had major damage, displacing hundreds of thousands of people.

Kate Hale, then Miami-Dade County director of emergency preparedness, was frustrated with the slow federal response. The *St. Petersburg Times* reported, "Three days after the storm, Hale and other top county officials met to discuss the dire situation. There were reports of desperate mothers dipping baby bottles in mud puddles. Residents sat in the wreckage of their homes holding shotguns to ward off looters. Police warned of violence unless food and shelter arrived. The officials agreed Hale would make a loud complaint at a news conference" (Adair 2002, p. A1). Hale's complaint was indeed vehement: "Where the hell is the cavalry on this one? We need food. We need water. We need people. For God's sake, where are they?" As she later recalled, "The game plan was 'Let Kate do it and if anybody gets offended we will fire her'"; she accordingly told her staff, "It's been nice working with you" (Adair 2002, p. A1). As agency spokesperson, Kate Hale was at once a victim of the storm, a crisis responder, and a scapegoat for the agency.

Agencies represent themselves through their spokespersons and often reach out to the public after a crisis via the press conference. First responders such as EMTs, firefighters, and police officers are the first faces that the victims see on the scene. Spokespeople are the first faces that the public sees. They, too, are part of the crisis response process and must engage in emotional labor to get their job done just as the police, EMTs, and firefighters must in order to do the technical aspects of the job. Here it is clear that the agency—embodied by Hale—was exhausted and frustrated with the progress of relief efforts, whether her own home was actually damaged or not. Whether she was a direct victim of the storm or not, she had to act as though she were. What do spokespersons say and how do they say it in order to convey competence and generate a sense of trust? The spokesperson is not only distant from the crisis emotionally, but usually distant from the situation physically as well, relying on reports from the field to craft her remarks. But at center stage, she must appear deeply involved and close to the situation. A person in this role must manage the tension of being an outsider (Lee 2001) who does not react to crises directly but who must speak on behalf of the agency and "maintain [its] credibility in the face of crisis" (Jarret 2007, p. 14).

This chapter focuses on the job of public information officers (PIOs) and crisis spokespersons in order to identify the emotive skills inherent in this work. We include PIOs and crisis spokespersons in our study of emotional labor and crisis response because they are a key part of the response process and their work presents its own set of unique emotional labor demands. PIOs are not typical first responders, not in the same way we think about fire, police, and emergency medical services. They are not at the scene, but must *act* as though they were. They are not firefighters or EMTs, but they have to speak with authority as though they were, or at least conjure the legitimacy in order to gain the trust of others and be considered competent enough to be the face of the department. Furthermore, theirs is, for the most part, one-way communication. They have to *be* the face of the department and act like they were at the scene of the crisis, all without gauging the effect of their message in real time, as other crisis responders can. Responding first and fast to a crisis, whether as a PIO or another first responder, requires a range of emotive skills. This chapter explores those skills inherent to the work of crisis spokespersons.

We are interested in understanding how this work is performed within the dynamic context of emergency and disaster response and in a world of instant communication. We examine how PIOs manage the media, navigate the press conference, and use it to frame meaning. We then address how PIOs communicate competence and cultivate trust, and their role in ongoing agency communications. We conclude that public relations and the job of the agency spokesperson is fundamentally about "human relations" and the art of translating "just the facts" into a message of competence, care, and concern in the relationship of the state to the citizenry.

Public Information Officers as the "Voice" of Government

Communication is a crucial aspect of governance (Waldo 1992, p. xi). The government has the obligation to keep all citizens adequately informed (Hiebert & Spitzer 1968). Public relations has been variously defined as the management of communications between an organization and its publics (Grunig & Hunt 1984); the means by which an administrator interacts with the citizenry and is held accountable; the interplay between commentators who report on crises for organizations, political and agency representatives, PIOs, and the media (Garnett & Kouzmin 2007); and "the art of adjusting organizations to environments and environments to organizations" (Crable & Vibbert 1986, p. 413). The principal aim is to attain, maintain, or enhance cooperation and consensus between an agency and its environment (Ehling 1992). The contemporary practice of public relations is about developing and maintaining relationships with publics (Grunig, Grunig, & Ehling 1992; Grunig, Grunig, & Dozier 2002). Its foundations include a people orientation, a value orientation, integrity, and communication (Daugherty 2001).

One category within this general rubric is *public reporting*, which entails post hoc reporting from the agency to the public at large, and press relations (Lee 2001). Public reporting, external communication, and publicity to accomplish democratic accountability are inherent in the activities of government agencies and public managers (Lee 2001; Viteritti 1997). The information officer is crucial to the government process (Hiebert & Spitzer 1968). Public information practitioners are journalists-in-residence who disseminate accurate, but usually only favorable, information about their organizations (Heath 2001). They communicate not as individuals but as institutional representatives (Banks 1995). A police department spokesperson illustrates:

> I'm in charge of public information. Basically our job is to communicate through the media and through other means with the citizens, and that responsibility is to keep them informed of potential hazards, dangers, things that are of interest, what the police department's doing. And there's a second role to the citizens where I actually market the police department to them, partly because it helps when the image of the police department is a good image. It helps in terms of getting information back that ultimately is taking people off the street that shouldn't be there or keeping people on the streets that should be. Communication and marketing, so to speak.

The fundamental goal of public reporting is to get agency or department information out to the citizenry (Morgan 1986) and to manage the accuracy and consistency of the messages coming from the agency (Coombs 1999). As such, the PIO is at the nexus of a public agency and the news media, serving as liaison between them (Lee 2001). Given the increasing importance of media in public affairs and civic society and the media's increasingly antibureaucratic stance, the PIO is becoming a crucial link between administrators and the public (Kovach & Rosenthal 1999; Lee 2001). There is a wider spectrum of media today, insisting that answers and explanations be given more quickly and more completely than ever before (Laitin 1980). If we agree that our government rests ultimately on public opinion, then the channel to the public is the PIO.

Crisis communication raises the stakes for the agency spokesperson. The claim that most disasters are really "local disasters" (Sylves & Waugh 1990, p. xiii) reminds us that, for the great majority of emergencies and disasters, local government is the first and only operational responder through a fire department, police department, or other agency (NAPA 1993). Interorganizational communication focuses on the allocation of resources and coordination of action among all stakeholders—government agencies, police and fire departments, rescue units, hospitals, health specialists, relief agencies, emergency management personnel—and interactions with other networks involved in the crisis. Coordinating crisis operations is a "complex process of multiple organizations within multiple networks debating options, exchanging information, and negotiating which actions to take" (Garnett & Kouzmin 2007, p. 180). Such is the milieu in which the PIO functions.

A crisis is the time when communicating is more difficult yet most essential (Garnett 1992). A growing body of scholarship attests to the crucial roles that communication plays in successful crisis management (Garnett & Kouzmin 2007). Most of the time, crisis situations turn out to be information and communication crises (Pijnenburg & van Duin 1991). Crises can be regarded as "information-poor" situations (Coombs 1999), as was the case with Hurricane Katrina in 2005. Given that we live in an "era of crises" (Lerbringer 1977, p. 3) in a "risk society" (Beck 1992, p. 9), crisis communication situations are ubiquitous, including crises or disasters involving whole communities, regions, or nations, and also emergency authorities in local accidents (Falkheimer & Heide 2006). Hurricane Andrew in 1992; the Oklahoma City bombing in 1995; the September 11 attacks in New York in 2001; the 2004 Indian Ocean tsunami; earthquakes in China in 2008, Indonesia in 2009, Haiti and Chile in 2010; and, in the same year, the unprecedented British Petroleum oil spill in the Gulf of Mexico; the catastrophic flooding in Pakistan in 2010; and the

Chilean mine collapse in 2010 are just a handful of recent crises that engaged the PIO.

Unlike any other jobholder in an agency, the PIO faces unique challenges that draw on one's adeptness at exercising emotional labor and artful affect. Mordecai Lee (2001, pp. 113, 122) raises three scenarios that demand emotional labor and are unique to the PIO:

- What about the classic situation when full and complete candor with the media is not in the agency's best interests?
- At the heart of the role of the PIO is "deniability" . . . is it better to be fully informed of internal agency deliberations or left in the dark?
- [T]o whom does the local spokesperson assign ultimate loyalty when confronted with professional dilemmas . . . to the agency itself, to the agency head, [or] to . . . professional standards[?]

Effective media relations are more art than science. Communication in government is more than a technical process of adhering to the mechanics of grammar and style (Garnett 1992). "There's an art to it" (Hiebert & Spitzer 1968, p. 309):

> The public information officer who compiles meticulously all the facts of a complex government undertaking and then callously inflicts it on a reporter is not helping anyone. He is like an artist painting a brick wall who feels compelled to draw the outline of every brick—until a viewer's eyes swim in confusion. The information officer should, instead, be like the artist who, by a cross-hatching here and there, suggests the brick of the wall. He should be able to select from a mass of fact those details that are significant and illustrative, which in a news story can give the reader the picture succinctly and clearly.

Zorthian goes a step further: "press relations is an art, not a science, and precise formulae cannot be applied" (1970, p. 42). Multiplicity and diversity of messages and audiences, greater politicization, heightened public scrutiny, more rigid legal restrictions, and a need for confidentiality balanced against the public's right to know—all these elements combine and interact to make government communication more necessary and more difficult than in the private sector. It requires the ability to analyze audiences and flexibility in communicating with them; good communicators are skillful diagnosticians, sizing up key factors in a situation and acting accordingly (Garnett 1992). A PIO of a major urban police department provides an illustration:

> The other set of challenges that I have in this office is [that] I'm dealing with community groups. I'm dealing with the news media from the local, state, national, and international level and that in itself poses challenges because it's one message or two messages; part of the challenge is fashioning it in a way that speaks to multiple audiences.

Agency spokespeople project the facts and feelings of their organizations. Goffman (1981) refers to the person who physically performs the communicative act of face-to-face interaction as an animator, suggesting the emotive aspects involved in adding "liveliness" to the exchange. There is no single right or best way to communicate in all government situations. Rather, appropriate ways to communicate depend upon the audience, sender, situation, objectives for communicating, medium, and message (Garnett 1992). In crisis situations, formal rules and procedures give way to informal processes and improvisation (Rosenthal, Charles, & Hart 1989). Flexibility is vital in postcrisis communication because no single approach will work for all crises (Seeger, Sellnow, & Ulmer 2001). A former deputy press secretary to the president of the United States explains (Laitin 1980, p. 14):

> I don't have a checklist, like an airline pilot for his pre-takeoff and pre-landing ritual, because every situation has to be dealt with as a separate problem. There are no pat answers. In an emergency, I have no emergency procedures for the simple reason that every emergency has a different character and a different cast of players . . . as a practitioner of a very imprecise art, I have no tablets of stone to hand down. I suggest only that government information people sensitize their fingertips to the problems of dealing with the public. They are there to be served.

An agency spokesperson has a pivotal role to play in crafting, delivering, interpreting, making sense of, and translating the facts into a message that conveys competence and compassion, serves to console and counsel, and instills public confidence and trust. During each phase of a disaster, the role of spokespersons (in concert with the media) follows a pattern. They give public information on what local government is doing to mitigate or prepare for the disaster. In the response phase, they communicate the basic information about what happened (the what, when, where, why, and how information about the crisis) and relay warning messages and all-clear signals to the public. In the containment and recovery phase, they give citizens information on where they can go for shelter and sustenance after a local disaster (Burkhart 1991).

But the pattern can take on very different shapes. For example, PIOs can blunt the negative impact of a damaging story by the way they handle it, the approach they take, and the attitude they show (Zorthian 1970). As one crisis manager puts it, how the news media view the PIO's coping skills will often set the tone for the entire crisis and shape the final image of what has happened. "Perception becomes reality" (Berry 1999, p. 9). The goal is to raise citizens' consciousness as well as faith, trust, and confidence in government (Jarret 2007). When Hurricane Katrina devastated the Gulf coast, federal officials failed to communicate the proper tone for handling the crisis. "Much of the public tone communicated by [them] was one of 'being in control' rather than showing appropriate engagement" that fosters trust and builds community (Garnett & Kouzmin 2007, p. 174).

But how is "appropriate engagement" expressed on the job, especially in crisis situations? The message that government cares about what has happened to people because of the crisis, that efforts are under way to cope with the crisis, and that the public needs to take certain steps to minimize damage and help government efforts is key (Garnett 1992). An agency must both establish control and show compassion during a crisis. Of these twin dimensions of credibility, control is consistent with expertise, and compassion is consistent with trustworthiness. A spokesperson for Florida's state emergency response team provides an illustration:

> It took a little time to get myself together [after an incident in which a firefighter was lost]. But I know that people will be focusing on me and my emotions and what I'm saying as to, okay, is this somebody who knows what's going on. I have to convey that message to them and explain to them what has happened, what's taking place and what's going to happen whether it's good or bad. . . . They could see the hurt and the pain that you have. . . . When it comes to other cases—children . . . I just talk to [the parents] as if I was talking to them without a camera so they know there's sincerity in what I'm saying. I'm talking also as a parent, and I will let them know that as well, that I'm a parent and this is some of the things that I would be feeling, and I would try to convey that to them.

The need for both control and compassion place particular demands on crisis communications (Coombs 1999). For people whose lives have been disrupted or who are in shock, symbols of competent caring on the part of their government are extremely important (NAPA 1993). As we have seen with the events of September 11, 2001, governments suffer if they exhibit apathy (Jarret 2007). President George W. Bush's lack of emotional reaction to the news of the World Trade Center attacks, former New York mayor Rudolf Giuliani's personal embrace of the tragedy, and the more recent criticism of President Barack Obama's reported "lawyerly and passive" (Milbank 2010) response to the British Petroleum oil spill in the Gulf of Mexico illustrate how the media's portrayal can shape public perception. How do agency spokespersons relate to the media with appropriate engagement that has both practical and symbolic value?

Managing the Media: The Role of the Press Conference

Never let them see you sweat.—Sharon Berry

The agency spokesperson, or public information officer, faces unique emotional labor demands when conducting a press conference held immediately after a crisis. The PIO seeks orderly responses to a disorderly environment (Heath 2001). Although crises produce tremendous surprise and uncertainty, the media and other stakeholders demand an immediate, thorough, and unqualified response from their government (Seeger et al. 2001). The spokesperson must rise above technique and manage the public relations and organizational communication function (Dozier 1992).

Press agentry/publicity and public information are one-way modes of communication. Although agency spokespersons may take questions from reporters, press conferences generally involve one-way communication. Their approach is more monologue than dialogue. In addition to several cognitive (technical) skills demanded of agency spokespersons, Jarret (2007, p. 16) adds several more affective abilities:

> The spokesperson should be . . . able to establish credibility with the media; able to project confidence to the audience; suitable in regard to diction and appearance; sincere, straightforward, and believable; accessible to the media and to internal communications personnel who will facilitate media interviews; and able to remain calm in stressful situations.

How do organizational representatives make their audience think that they, and by extension their agency, are credible, confident, sincere, accessible, and calm? How do they engender a positive image of their agency to a mostly cynical and distrusting public who adhere to "archetypal stories" of an "uncaring government" and of the public administrator as a "martinet who is rigidly applying a regulation or requirement instead of making an exception based on decency and reasonableness?" (Lee 1999, p. 455). How do they cultivate the perceptions of control and compassion? What are the most effective ways to inform the population about, for example, changes in the level of a threat without generating either complacency or excessive and counterproductive fear? (Foa et al. 2005). The answers lie in the emotive skills of the agency spokesperson.

Whether the role is one of expert prescriber, communication facilitator, problem-solving process facilitator, or communication technician (Dozier 1992), PIOs do more than share information. They build, nurture, and manage face-to-face relationships (Cropp & Pincus 2001). Impression management,[1] or self-presentation, including self-discipline, and self-impression skills are key (Rosenfeld & Giacalone 1991; Pohl & Vandeventer 2001). While impression management alone may not be sufficient to cope with a crisis, most politicians and administrators agree that it is indispensable (Rosenthal et al. 1989). Poor delivery skills are often interpreted as signs of deception (Coombs 1999). How the spokesperson reports to the public is as important as what is reported (Lee 1999). The public seldom judges an agency by facts, but rather on what it perceives to be facts, based on emotions evoked by the PIO's performance in the spotlight (Berge 1990). A spokesperson for a large municipal fire department explains:

> I try to paint a picture for viewers and listeners of what is going through the mind of the firefighter or the first responder that pulled the baby out, was just involved in that car crash, was working on the plane crash . . . so that they can express themselves in a first-person manner—what they saw, smelled, felt—to try and best evoke their feelings through my choice of words to the population . . . adding emphasis to something I felt that firefighter feels. If that firefighter had such a sorrowful face on I would try to describe the sorrow that I saw on that firefighter the moment he or she was explaining to me what he or she went through. So it was an ability to feel the pain or the suffering or the emotions of that rescuer and being able to translate that to an articulate sentence or paragraph or sound bite that people could associate with.

Press conferences are not slow-moving events. Answering questions demands the ability to think quickly and answer questions rapidly. "No comment" is usually not a viable option, since it raises the danger that stakeholders hear "we're guilty" instead of "no comment." It is also a form of silence, a very passive response (Coombs 1999, p. 116). A police department PIO provides insight:

> If it's something that we can't talk about, then we don't talk about it. . . . I represent all seven hundred members of the department . . . so my goal is to make sure that everything comes out correct, it comes out right and if it isn't right then I will tell you it's not, and if I don't know the answer then I find out and get back to them as soon as possible so they don't feel like, okay, well, we're being avoided or they don't want to answer the questions because then that turns right back to me. The PIO's always the one that ends up getting the brunt of the beatings.

The spokesperson is expected to be "cordial" and should not exhibit verbal aggressiveness or argumentativeness (Coombs 1999, p. 76). PIOs should be effective, enthusiastic, and passionate. Zorthian presents the rules of engagement as three commandments (1970, pp. 41–42):

1. No lying to the press;
2. Restrict security to an absolute minimum; and
3. Take the initiative in getting out a story, even a negative one, in your terms, under conditions of your choosing, and in a setting that you've helped to set up.

Media spokesperson training typically focuses on three responsibilities: be an educator, be quotable, and be prepared (Zorthian 1970). Compounding this responsibility is the fact that spokespeople do their job in times of high stress: there is a crisis, and the media want answers immediately (Coombs 1999). A fascinating example of spokesperson training comes to us from an unexpected source at the time of this writing. In October 2010, thirty-three men who had been trapped thousands of feet underground in a Chilean mine for more than two months were about to be rescued, and "with as many as two thousand journalists waiting for them on the surface, the first thing they asked for was media training." The *Toronto Star* reported that "a former journalist was provided to run through questions with them" to "get the story straight" (Kelly 2010). As the *Guardian UK* reported, "They have lived through a catastrophic mine collapse and survived for nearly two months underground, but now the trapped Chilean miners are preparing for a fresh ordeal: surviving the attention of the world's media above ground" (Franklin 2010).

The miners became spokespersons for the state. Because the whole world was watching and mining provides nearly forty percent of state earnings, Chilean president Sebastian Pinera "put his mining minister and the operations chief of state-owned Codelco, the country's biggest [mining] company, in charge of the rescue" (CBS/AP 2010). These thirty-three men were thrust onto the international stage and became the faces and voices of the nation. Their words could not be subject to their emotions; their message was shaped and orchestrated in the interests of the state. They were taught to encode a message and to know their audience as impromptu representatives of an entire nation.

"Encoding" skills (devising a message), "sender" skills (writing, speaking, body language), and "receiver" skills (the importance of knowing audiences and the receiving process before a message can be intelligently crafted and sent, including making adjustments in response to what one is hearing) are all in play, with "audience analysis" a key component (Garnett 1992, p. xvii–21, 42). Because the goals of media relations include avoiding conflict with key constituents, bringing about positive changes in relationships with key publics, and collaborative advocacy when attempting to survive a crisis, it follows that conflict management, negotiation, relationship-building (maintenance and enhancement), and developing rapport are essential job skills (Grunig et al. 2002). These are emotive skills.

Media relations are human relations. While mass media and high-tech communications are increasingly being used by government, much communication surrounding crises remains face-to-face, oral, and nuanced whether at the scene of the crisis or in a command center used by the crisis team (Comfort & Cahill 1988; Garnett 1992; Garnett & Kouzmin 2007). "The key to effective, appealing government reporting is the people factor. First, tell the news of government through people. Second, relate news of government to people" (Killenberg 1992, p. 127). But it involves more than that, especially in crisis situations. "Because we are dealing with human complexity, the communication system will have to be designed to accommodate humans" (D'Aprix 1988, p. 270). And it will require spokespersons who are skilled in the art of emotive (human) relations. We turn next to the role of PIOs in using the press conference to frame meaning. How do they summarize and shape the public's interpretation of events? How does this happen via one-way communication in a press conference? What are the consequences of failure?

How PIOs Frame Meaning

PIOs frame meaning within the context of the event: sometimes they build the frame themselves; sometimes they engage in damage control and meaning-making within a frame of others' creation. Matt Welch's 2005 article "They Shoot Helicopters, Don't They?" is subtitled "How Journalists Spread Rumors during Katrina," and in it he describes how meanings were made, unmade, and remade in the days following Hurricane Katrina (Welch 2005, p. 18):

> On September 1, 2005, seventy-two hours after Hurricane Katrina ripped through New Orleans, the Associated Press news wire flashed a nightmare of a story: "Katrina Evacuation Halted Amid Gunfire, Shots Fired at Military Helicopter." The article flew across the globe via at least one hundred and fifty news outlets, from India to Turkey to Spain. Within twenty-four hours commentators on every major American television news network had helped turn the helicopter sniper image into the disaster's enduring symbol of dysfunctional urbanites too depraved to be saved. . . . Like many early horror stories about ultra-violent New Orleans natives, whether in their home city or in far-flung temporary shelters, the AP article turned out to be false.

It was against this backdrop that representatives from the Federal Emergency Management Agency (FEMA), the U.S. Coast Guard, and the National Guard addressed the public. Agency spokespersons can affect how the public perceives a crisis by how they frame it when they present it. A frame is the meaning one attaches to the problem when presenting it. A frame affects interpretations of the problem by highlighting certain of its features while masking others (Coombs 1999). Media coverage helps frame the expectations and judgments of citizens, reporters, and politicians (Morgan 1986). PIOs must have information to support the frame and articulate it in a compelling fashion. Frame development begins with information, for example, that indicates a crisis is important, immediate, or uncertain (Coombs 1999). A successful agency spokesperson is effective at interacting with the media at the definition-setting stage of media coverage (Lee 1999). According to Luke (1999, p. 626), "How an issue is reported has significant impact on how the problem is initially characterized or framed. Once an issue has been described in one way early in the issue attention cycle, it is difficult for individuals to reframe the issue to a different perspective."

Framing meaning is not the sole purview of the PIO. The role of the media, particularly television, shapes the way in which other journalists and audiences "frame" the crisis to form the "myth of the story," which, in turn, shapes the way journalists report the crisis and how the public perceives it (Garnett & Kouzmin 2007, p. 176). Nevertheless, PIOs provide the framework for the development and evolution of the story (Zorthian 1970). In dealing with any kind of crisis, the PIO first has to get the facts straight: What has happened, what is the agency going to do about it, and what does the future hold (Berge 1990)?

That first sound bite or headline very often sets the tone. The first twenty-four hours are decisive, as external perceptions are established quickly. Once they are in place, it is difficult to shake them. With respect to the Hurricane Katrina helicopter incident, U.S. Coast Guard spokeswoman Jolie Shifflet probably would have preferred to highlight the fact that the Coast Guard rescued more than 33,000 people, but instead she was left deflecting rumors: "Coast Guard helicopters were not fired on during Hurricane Katrina rescue operations" (Welch 2005, p. 1).

A quick response is necessary to get the organization's definition of the crisis—its side of the story—into the media and out to the stakeholders. A quick response also helps to create the impression of control (Coombs 1999). Believability is essential during any type of crisis. Our respondents repeatedly referred to an antagonistic relationship and the need for "controlling the media rather than the media controlling you," as the following vignette illustrates:

I don't let anybody jackpot me. They'll try to jackpot you. They'll try to get you to say something that you shouldn't. . . . [You need to] control the message, don't let them control you . . . give me three good points to go with. Just give me three things and they'll be happy. But the main thing is don't bullshit, stay on point, if they come at you from the left and you don't know, say I don't know the answer but if I do, I'll let you know. Control it like that. Don't let them control you.

Issues management is a systematic approach intended to shape how the issue develops and is resolved. It is a proactive attempt to have an issue decided in a way favorable to an organization (Coombs 1999). People are persuaded by three basic factors: emotion, reason, and credibility. Emotion centers on how the message is presented. Spokespersons who use emotions to capture the public's attention can then use compelling rational evidence to support the acceptance of the crisis (Coombs 1999). Reactions can be made worse if the story is sensationalized in the media and if there is poor transfer of specific recommendations by public officials (Foa et al. 2005). This was the case with Hurricane Katrina. The consequences of these failures continue to reverberate today. The next two sections focus on how PIOs communicate competence and cultivate trust—both absent during the Katrina tragedy.

How PIOs Communicate Competence

In its report, the [House Select] committee characterized the response to Katrina as a "litany of mistakes, misjudgments, lapses, and absurdities all cascading together, blinding us to what was coming and hobbling any collective effort to respond."
—Dwight Ink

The short answer to the question of how to communicate competence is, with feeling. Competence is conveyed by an agency spokesperson's skill in technique and affect. Emotive skills come into play in reading the audience, tailoring the message to fit the circumstances, making judgments about how much information to deliver, and managing the delivery. Our respondents emphasized the need to project a voice of calm, control, honesty, and authority and to "keep it simple" by avoiding "computerese, bureaucratese, officialese, and legalese" (Garnett 1992, p. 29).

I talk to people the way I would want them to talk to me. You know, I don't use big words. I don't try to fill their heads with something that may lead them to believe what I say and that may not be the truth. . . . My mom has always taught us, you know, treat people the way you would want to be treated, and you talk to them with the same level of respect, and that's what I do, and I think that has really taken me a long way in the five years that I've been doing this.

A crisis situation will inevitably affect the feelings and behaviors of victims and people trying to resolve it. Tension, frustration, fatigue, worry, and grief can be expected, especially during severe or long crises. PIOs can help in such situations by exhibiting at least the impression of calm and by avoiding remarks or actions likely to threaten or antagonize people unnecessarily (Garnett 1992), as the following vignette illustrates:

> When speaking to the public, I would try to be a conveyor of information. I would try to show empathy. I would try to show concern. When I spoke to large groups through bulletins at the top of the hour or when I was speaking to one-on-one camera interviews, I tried to make it clear that I was speaking as the regular Joe next door—the regular neighbor but because of what I am doing I had some information that may help you. I find that people, folks, general population like to hear things simply and like to hear things to the point as best you can.

Crafting the appropriate tone of the message can build rapport and credibility with audiences. Tone is how a message "sounds" to an audience (Garnett 1992, p. 80). An agency spokesperson is "not merely the passive recipient of role-sending, but to a greater or lesser degree modifies the role and the expectations of the role-set by the manner of role enactment" (Katz & Kahn 1978, p. 208). An understanding of the "silent language" of behavior and cultural differences is part of the emotive skills inventory (Hall 1981, p. 1). Public relations communications will be accepted as reflecting reality only if they harmonize with the cultural experience of audiences (Banks 1995, p. 40). A PIO's ignorance of, or indifference to, verbal and nonverbal cues can result in an unsatisfactory interview and a botched story (Killenberg 1992). A fire chief provides an illustration:

> Something like this doesn't happen in anybody's lifetime where you have four kids killed, a car driving through [during the opening day of Little League], here's the worst nightmare. . . . I was the face of the village . . . from the time of the call until about eleven o'clock at night, that's all I did was talk to the media . . . the police chief and his lieutenant were absolutely a disaster. Couldn't talk, couldn't respond properly, wouldn't answer the questions, became belligerent. . . . They were absolutely making a disgrace.

Bad news conveyed sensitively and artfully still may be difficult to accept. If conveyed poorly, bad news can be disastrous. A cardinal principle in relating negative news is for PIOs to communicate such news the way they would want to get it themselves, with respect and sensitivity (Garnett 1992). A PIO of a major urban police department illustrates:

> There's the challenge of getting them to accept that even when the medicine that you're giving is not very tasty, it's the right medicine.

Speaking in "harmony with the audience" also requires an understanding that the line between victims and nonvictims is not as obvious as might appear at first glance. Beyond those who have been hurt physically or have incurred losses of possessions is a wide variety of "hidden victims," including emergency personnel—rescuers—and family members of victims (Drabek 1986, p. 273). And beyond these secondary victims with affected family and friends are tertiary victims—the general citizenry who may show severe stress reactions (Foa et al. 2005). Accuracy and consistency of message also convey competence. Speaking "with one voice" (Coombs 1999, p. 117) is facilitated by having one individual designated as the primary spokesperson to represent the community, make official statements, and answer media questions (Jarret 2007). Having one clear voice in crisis communication means controlling the messages an organization gives publics by funneling all communication through a single speaker (Banks 1995).

How PIOs Cultivate Trust

> *In this and like communities public sentiment is everything.*
> *With public sentiment, nothing can fail. Without it, nothing can*
> *succeed. Consequently, he who moulds public sentiment goes*
> *deeper than he who enacts statutes and pronounces decisions.*
> —Abraham Lincoln

Abraham Lincoln said those words in 1858, which is a testament to the timelessness of the need for trustworthy public information. Trust is of major importance in crisis communication. If citizens do not trust authorities and their spokespersons, it is very hard to reach and influence them during a crisis (Falkheimer & Heide 2006). But agency spokespersons walk a fine line as they navigate between the competing demands of full public disclosure from a public relations perspective and limited disclosure of crisis-related information from a legal perspective (Coombs 1999). PIOs may feel pressure to tell something less than the whole story, but they also have a duty to provide the facts. Lee speaks about this tension in terms of conflicting loyalties (2001, p. 122):

Given the conflicting pressures of the press, the agency, the appointed agency head, the legislative body, and the chief elected official, to whom does the local spokesperson assign ultimate loyalty when confronted with professional dilemmas? What about the classic situation when full and complete candor with the media is not in the agency's best interest?

Deniability is a related dilemma for a PIO and relates to addressing matters that are not yet public. Lee (2001) asks whether it is better for the PIO to be fully informed of internal agency deliberations or left in the dark. Regardless of the answer, trust is cultivated when PIOs craft their message with the audiences' experience in mind, facilitating interaction that "affirms audience members' identities, honors their interests, reckons with their cultural orientations, and listens actively to their arguments" (Banks 1995, p. 98). In other words, there is trust when the spokesperson develops rapport with participants. This is central to communicating effectively with audiences during crises: "Rapport among people is most necessary during crisis, precisely when rapport is most likely to be stretched thin or missing altogether" (Garnett 1992, p. 217).

Trust is a complicated concept that has several underlying dimensions. One of these is integrity, the belief that an agency is fair and just. A second is dependability, the belief that an agency will do what it says it will do. A third is competence, the belief that an agency has the ability to do what it says it will do (Grunig et al. 2002). As the agency spokesperson, the PIO is expected to model and articulate these values on the job, during the emotional intensity of crisis situations.

Credibility is an important concept because it has a significant effect on the persuasiveness of a message. As Coombs explains (1999, p. 46), "Credibility can be divided into two components, expertise and trustworthiness. Expertise is the communicator's knowledge about the subject. Trustworthiness is the communicator's goodwill toward or concern for the receivers." McCroskey (1998, p. 215) identifies three types of credibility:

Initial credibility is the credibility the communicator has before he or she speaks. Derived credibility is the credibility produced by the communicator's message. Terminal credibility is the credibility after the communicator has spoken and represents a combination of initial and derived credibility.

Compassion is linked to credibility as well. The compassion of an agency indicates that it is trustworthy and is concerned about the needs of its stakeholders. Concern is an accepted part of trustworthiness, as are candor, realism, and honesty (Coombs 1999; Hiebert & Spitzer 1968). According to Garnett (1992, p. 230), "Truth in communicating involves accuracy, avoiding falsehood or misrepresentation whether by including false information, deliberately excluding vital information, or deliberately allowing people to misinterpret a message. To have the most value, however, truth in communicating needs to include usefulness, openness, and fairness as well as accuracy."

Agency spokespersons judged trustworthy (expert, experienced, and unbiased) can produce several times the opinion-change that communicators with little credibility can produce (Garnett 1992). A crisis spokesperson describes the nuances of communicating "truth":

> I've never lied but I haven't [always told the complete truth]. I knew we had a fatal fire and I knew the woman had already expired and the news [asked about] her condition, I said she's in very critical condition because I'm not going to tell the family on the ten o'clock news tonight that their family member is dead. So I guess in the sense that would be a lie so I guess I have lied when I think about it, but not intentionally.

In fact, the spokesperson's statement was "a little white lie" told to prevent the next of kin from hearing of the death on the nightly news. This choice was made to protect the victim's family when no harm was done by delaying the truth. It was a decision made by the spokesperson. In many such cases, PIOs know more than they can tell and have to make a decision about how much information to give. The next vignette from a fellow spokesperson provides another illustration:

> We lost a fireman in 1989 and that was probably the toughest point in my career because we had a fire . . . Joe was the last one [out of the burning basement]. He turned around to make sure everyone was out, the mortar collapsed and down he went and he died, and we couldn't find his wife . . . and I put a gag order on everybody, but the news media picked up on this man. Now the family hadn't been notified yet. I'm [at the hospital] with one of the nurses and one of the [media] guys comes . . . I say what can I help you with? [He said that Joe was] killed in the line of duty. [I said] you got misinformation—sorry, and walked away. And so we finally found his wife. Got her in there, broke the news to her. And then [the reporter] told me he wanted information, he even spelled [Joe's name] wrong. I don't care. We're not giving you anything before the family's been notified.

> *Interviewer: What if he hadn't misspelled it? Would you have lied?*

> I wouldn't have lied. I would just say I don't know if your information is correct. That's all I would have said. So it just so happened that he had the

spelling wrong and we had information that was incorrect. So I got out of that one.

The case of Hurricane Katrina provides an indelible illustration of how a lack of trust in communication enabled rumor to thrive, including the urban legend of hurricane survivors shooting at Coast Guard helicopters. Truth became a casualty (Welch 2005, p. 18).

Ongoing Agency Communications

You never want to speak your own opinion because what can happen is that can bite you. You've got to be very careful.
—Police Chief

Jarret (2007, p. 14) underscores the importance of maintaining an ongoing public presence rather than appearing in front of cameras only when something has gone wrong: "Once the crisis occurs, most of your time will be spent communicating with citizens and the media—not a good time to attempt to educate anyone. Attempting to do so will seem like 'doublespeak.'" Agencies educate the citizenry by publicizing their policies, practices, and plans of action. Cultivating competence and trust is an ongoing agency function (Jarret 2007, p. 16): "Any efforts your local government has exerted in an effort to raise citizen consciousness as well as faith, trust, and confidence in government will be for naught if it is perceived that the government's own rules, regulations, policies and procedures are the problem and not the solution."

Summary

Trust, compassion, rapport, credibility. All these attributes hinge on the ability of the PIO to convey a message in a meaningful, understandable, tempered way. Because press conferences often occur at the height of a crisis, the spokesperson must control personal emotion while focusing on the facts of the matter.

Communication is a mission-critical agency function. Public information officers bear the greatest responsibility for managing others' perceptions of the agency's preparedness for crisis and its competence in the face of crisis. Communication is essential to shortening the duration of the crisis because it is at the heart of the initial response, strengthening reputational management, informing stakeholders, and providing follow-up information. The message allows the crisis team to reestablish a sense of organizational control over events and express compassion for victims (Coombs 1999). How PIOs communicate with their publics can have positive or negative outcomes. Done well, PIOs project agency competence and cultivate trust. They do so by managing their emotions at the same time as they take the emotional pulse of their audiences and adjust their manner and tone accordingly. Like other first responders and emergency services personnel, public information officers are part of the crisis response process, and their emotional labor demands are unique. Their work is more art than science and more about "human relations" than "just the facts."

Note

1. Impression management is usually defined as the deliberate attempts individuals make to influence the images that others form of them (Eden 1991, 17). It has to do with how people manage verbal and nonverbal communication to convey a positive image of themselves to others (Rahim & Buntzman 1991, 158).

5

Who Gets the Blame?
Who Gets the Credit?

Government Responsiveness
and Accountability

In *The Grapes of Wrath* (1939), John Steinbeck tells the story of desperately poor people living off the land in Oklahoma and their forced migration west. Generations of farming in Oklahoma, Kansas, and parts of Texas, New Mexico, and Colorado had depleted the soil so severely that the topsoil itself was drawn up into the wind and blown away. The result was black tornadoes of dirt and the Dust Bowl of the 1930s. Amid the Great Depression, the United States and state governments did what they could for the urban poor, but few resources were left for the rural poor scattered across the Great Plains. Most were left with no harbor of refuge to turn to. Even those who wanted to stay were forced out by the landowners, for the farmers were only sharecroppers after all. Poor, powerless, and without recourse to government support, these families supported themselves and each other on their way to new lives in California. The desperation of their condition produced a palpable expression of frustration, hopelessness, and the human need to assign blame in this classic passage about a shotgun-wielding sharecropper receiving eviction orders (Steinbeck 1939, p. 40):

> "Who gave you orders? I'll go after him. He's the one to kill."
> "You're wrong. He got his orders from the bank. The bank told him, 'Clear those people out or it's your job.'"
> "Well, there's a president of the bank. There's a board of directors. I'll fill up the magazine of the rifle and go into the bank."
> The driver said, "Fellow was telling me the bank gets orders from the East. The orders were, 'Make the land show a profit or we'll close you up.'"
> "But where does it stop? Who can we shoot?"

This passage is a classic depiction of human frustration with nameless, faceless bureaucracy—note that Steinbeck does not even give names to these characters—a frustration that is amplified in crisis situations. A deeply frustrated public often wants to know "who can we shoot?" Who is to blame? The previous chapter examined the role of agency spokespersons, and while they project the face and feelings of the organization, they are not usually held accountable for agency actions. This chapter focuses on the twin values of responsiveness and accountability and the inherent tensions between them. Our purpose is to map the contours of how accountability and responsiveness are sought and achieved within the context of the day-to-day work of crisis and emergency response. We are interested in understanding to whom workers are accountable, how they reconcile conflicting accountabilities, and what emotive skills they use in the process. We examine the many faces of accountability, including "accountability to" the citizenry as well as "accountability for" resources allocated from taxpayer dollars (Bardach & Lesser 1996). Preventing the potential abuse of power is the overarching goal of accountability arrangements, but these procedures also serve narrower purposes such as enhancing responsiveness (Thomas 1998).

The concept of responsiveness is related to, but different from the concept of accountability. Accountability and responsibility are often held to be synonymous: a reminder that one cannot be accountable to anyone, unless one also has responsibility *for* doing something (Day & Klein 1987). Simply stated, responsiveness entails responding readily and sympathetically to some request or signal from an outside source (Thomas 1998). Stivers expands this definition by the inclusion of "skillful listening" (1994, p. 367). Responsiveness relates upward to political or administrative officials as well as downward to citizens. We illustrate how difficult it is to achieve accountability and responsibility simultaneously because of the incompatible objectives of producing both control and discretion (Rockman 1998). We address the measurement of accountability in the dynamic environment of crisis response, and the relationship between responsiveness and accountability. We explore how crisis responders adapt their standard "rules of engagement" to exigencies on the scene (including level of risk, scope, scale, cultural contingencies, and physical and emotional capacity). The chapter closes by examining accountability and responsiveness in light of performance expectations.

First Responders' Burden as the "Face" of Government

> *We are the face of government. We do show up. We do represent government . . . and a lot of those people think they're there because of government or they're there because they've been*

put down . . . and when you walk in as a face of authority or government . . . you have to be careful. Fortunately for us in our profession, we're the good guys.

—Fire Rescue Captain

Responsiveness and accountability have nuanced meanings when applied to crisis situations. First-response organizations such as fire departments, emergency medical services, hospitals, police departments, and county rescue squads meet urgent demands of disaster victims under chaotic circumstances (Comfort, Ko, & Zagorecki 2004). Decisions are made in the moment as the trauma or disaster unfolds. First responders routinely function in chaotic situations, but chaos itself is a relative term. Law enforcement officers, for example, witness horrors that others do not see. Shootings, auto accidents, and battered families define the job (Herron 2001).

Responsiveness and accountability join together in practice. As the "face" of government, first responders and emergency services personnel carry a unique responsibility. They are the government, up close and personal, on the worst day of a citizen's life. Accountability is complicated particularly when employees face multiple sources of authority and competing expectations for performance (Romzek 2000). The concept of responsiveness is no less complex. Responsiveness to whom, for what, and in what form shape its practice. While the dilemma facing public administrators has traditionally been posed as a polarized choice between responsiveness to elected officials versus responsiveness to the public, the dilemma for first responders is more immediate and multidimensional during crisis response. The case of the 2010 earthquake in Haiti provides a case in point.

The human tragedy in the aftermath of the 7.0-magnitude earthquake in Haiti seemed never-ending. As with Hurricane Katrina in 2005, disaster victims relied on government to take the lead in coordinating the response and to rally local, national, and international donors and relief organizations. The images coming out of the capital of Port-au-Prince and the coastal city of Jacmel illustrated life and death, hope and despair, in stark relief. First responders became the lifeline: to a schoolgirl trapped beneath the rubble, to a pregnant woman rescued days later, to the dazed and bloodied father searching for his family. During a disaster, calculations of success and failure are fluid, and accountability, discretion, and responsiveness are bound together. Where should rescue efforts be focused? Which building to search first? Which victim to help? These same questions were asked in the aftermath of the 8.8-magnitude earthquake that struck Chile on February 27, 2010, and are asked again at each new disaster.

Where you stand determines what you see. This is the case when analyzing large-scale rescue efforts such as occurred in the aftermath of Hurricane

Katrina, when the levees broke in New Orleans and flooded countless homes. Stivers (2007) asserts that the work stories of first responders reveal moral judgments. (This is a matter of contention among responders: Law enforcement officials and social workers are likely to agree with her assessment while firefighters and EMTs beg to differ.) She concludes that rescue protocols sorted clients into three categories: those worthy of extraordinary help, those who got what the rules say and no more, and those who got no help. Stivers examined shirking on the job in the wake of Hurricane Katrina just as Adams, Balfour, and Reed (2006) profiled the unethical behavior of prison guards at Abu Ghraib prison in Iraq.

Less dramatic, but perhaps more important due to the opportunities for the exercise of creative discretion, Maynard-Moody and Musheno (2000) write about street-level service providers. They allege that workers sometimes base their decisions on their judgments about the worth of the individual citizen-client. Generously referred to as triage, discretion such as this has the effect of allocating resources to some while withholding them from others. Workers are put in a position to wonder whether clients are telling the truth or just "gaming the system" in order to gain goods and services for which they are not eligible. In this context, this work is a service dominated by the language of needs rather than of rights (Day & Klein 1987). Conversely, street-level workers are also in a position to act as "citizen-agents," being responsive and accountable to individuals and circumstances, rather than as pure "state-agents" adhering to the letter of the law. Without enough time or money to satisfy all needs, they ration it by judgment call, deciding not only who should be helped first, but who can be helped (Maynard-Moody & Musheno 2000).

In the case of emergency services, even the most dedicated and ethical rescuers must make heart-wrenching decisions about who receives care first. Despite the presence of a fairly clear-cut protocol for determining whom to treat first, every victim on the scene might want to be cared for first, but the training of responders requires them to assess the situation and determine who among all of the victims needs immediate care and who must wait. Even in the best situations, need exceeds resources. Decisions must be made. Even when using predetermined criteria, making those decisions without letting emotions get in the way is emotional labor.

A fire captain assigned to search-and-rescue work in Haiti refers to this process as "information triage" and "site triage." Information and intelligence must be sorted by degree of validity, and reconnaissance teams sort sites by their expectation of the number of "live finds" they will make. Professional norms and training present yet other choices. For health-care providers dealing with mass casualties, decisions are made according to a color-coded disaster triage process, in which patients are categorized as:

- Green—ambulatory patients who are safe,
- Yellow—patients with severe injuries who are hemo-dynamically stable,
- Red—patients who are considered to have significant life-threatening injuries, or
- Black—patients who are "unsalvageable."

These are high-stakes decisions involving individual discretion on the ground in a state of high uncertainty in the midst of chaos. The margin for error is slight (Comfort et al. 2004, p. 305). A *blind response* occurs when emergency squads enter a situation with little to no information. Responders arbitrarily start work wherever they can when they arrive on scene. A *time-based response* refers to dispatching first responders immediately upon receipt of the emergency call, on a first-come, first-served basis. In the third scenario, *severity-based response*, squads know when the call came in plus they know the severity of the incident. In such cases, severity is the dominant factor in determining action and allocating resources. How might "skillful listening" improve the odds that the response will be effective? Stivers (1994, p. 364) asks a complementary question: How can good listening help public servants be more responsive to the public?

> The experience of listening involves openness, respect for difference, and reflexivity. Developing the capacity to listen well promotes accountability by helping administrators to hear neglected voices and engage in recipro-cal communication with the public; it promotes effectiveness by deepen-ing our understanding of complex situations and facilitating imaginative approaches.

For Stivers, responsiveness *begins* with listening: "public institutions take their shape partly as a result of how people at the intercept between agency and environment listen to and respond to one another" (1994, p. 367). First responders are on the razor's edge of that intercept, which is further defined by Comfort (2002) as "the context that is most conducive to creative performance in living systems and hence most likely to generate innovative strategies in response to unexpected demands." Listening is crucial as it helps responders glean important information, define situations carefully, and take prudent action in a turbulent environment (Stivers 1994).

Responsiveness also exacts a toll on those who respond. For example, journalists reporting from the front lines of the Haiti earthquake revealed their struggle to reconcile the incompatible goals of filing their stories and, simultaneously, needing to help those about whom they were reporting. The emotional toll on those working at "the edge of chaos" can manifest itself in post-traumatic stress disorder (PTSD) and other physiological or psychological symptoms. Mitchell (1988) found that more than 86 percent of disaster workers experience some symptoms of PTSD within twenty-four hours after their experiences at the scenes of major emergencies. Approximately ten percent may be profoundly distressed by the event. They are unable to continue in that line of work, they experience a personality change, their marriages and family life are disturbed, or they become physically ill (1998). The burden of being the face of government can be overwhelming. Responding in these environments can be career-changing, even career-ending. A chief in the fire rescue domestic preparedness division speaks about "responding to New York" in the aftermath of September 11, 2001:

> We were deployed up there and that took me good two plus years to get past [it]. The pictures don't do it justice. But when you physically get up there and you get out and you see twenty-three acres of destruction and fires underground you know there's nothing you can do except volume recovery. . . . Other guys had problems from that for years.

A fire captain similarly describes his life before and after Hurricane Katrina in world-weary terms:

> Up until Hurricane Katrina I had been a figurehead for this department, the lead spokesperson. . . . My life was a very visible life. The events of Hurricane Katrina made me throw up my arms and say I'm ready for a change. I think I've seen enough. I think I've done enough. I'm tired. I think that's a symbolic moment of my life where I decided to try something different. And in that transition of about a year and a half from after Katrina, working downtown, I decided that *I just think I lived too much.*

A sense of fatalism and of the fragility of life is a common refrain as first responders describe their experiences. Their daily exposure to dangerous and life-threatening situations makes them "crispy." For example, the tragic consequences of crimes place an emotional burden on law enforcement officers as they try to make sense of things. This is particularly problematic when children are involved (Pogrebin & Poole 1991). The experience can hit close to home and become personalized:

> If you go to a call, and it doesn't make sense, like two kids that were beat with a bat and they were dead, just, it makes me in my own life realize, you know, there's evil people out there . . . there's a lot of sick people out there and they're crazy . . . and you will be the victim. . . . I've learned

from working here that people are very unpredictable. . . . Always love your relatives because it's less than a second. You could be sitting here and just stroke out.

Being the face of government can bring about a heightened sense of the responders' own mortality. For example, "hostage takings are one of the most difficult events for officers called to a scene because they can relate to it in terms of their own family. It brings them face-to-face with their own mortality" (Goss 2005, p. 51). An officer's expectations of personal infallibility become tempered by incidents such as an officer-involved shooting, the death of a coworker, exposure to a grisly crime scene, or a police suicide (Cross & Ashley 2004, p. 25).

Government responsiveness takes on a much richer meaning when we consider how this work must be performed under volatile, dangerous, and extraordinarily stressful conditions. In the following sections, we examine how workers do what they do within a framework of governmental accountability, a complementary and multifaceted term when applied in practice.

Accountability and Crisis Response

If you make a mistake, there's no do-overs.—Fire Rescue Chief

Accountability, like responsiveness, is a relational concept. Accountability, which has been characterized as the heart of governance in democratic societies (Thomas 1998), is founded in the Athenian concept of direct accountability to the people (Jones 1957; Roberts 1982). Its objective is to ensure that public administrators pursue publicly valued goals and satisfy legitimate performance expectations (Romzek & Dubnick 1998). As we explore below, accountability relations in governance are inherently complex. Service delivery has seen a growth of professionalism in emergency management, crisis response, and law enforcement (Day & Klein 1987). It has led to more and closer relations between the bureaucracy and citizen-clients. This, in turn, has produced increased need for citizen participation in decision making. And this affects accountability measures (Thomas 1998, p. 355):

> The contentious, vague, complex, multiple, shifting, and sometimes conflicting nature of the goals of many public organizations and public programs makes the fulfillment of the information requirements of a sound accountability framework far more difficult than for private firms.

The term "accountability" is generally understood as a "calling to account" for what public officials and their subordinates have or have not done (Stone

1995, p. 507). This refers to answerability for one's actions, behavior, or performance, with sanctions assessed in the event of unmet expectations. Like the concept of responsiveness, accountability raises questions: Accountable to whom? For what? And how? Are workers accountable to themselves, to citizens, to agency rules? How do workers reconcile conflicting accountabilities? What are the emotive skills and "head-games" they use in the process?

The answers to these questions are not simple. They go beyond mere oversight and reporting arrangements. This is especially the case in crisis response because discretion is inherent in this work and unpredictable exigencies modify each situation (Bardach & Lesser 1996). Norms, belief systems, and perceptions motivate responders to act. Firefighting and emergency medical services are held to an across-the-board standard that anyone in need will be served equally. But in many other types of response, such as law enforcement and street-level social services, there are intangibles that are "shadowy, never fully articulated, and often inconsistent" and "often subversive to formal authority and democratic accountability" (Maynard-Moody & Musheno 2000, p. 333).

Accountability to Whom?

First responders function within multiple, overlapping, and competing accountability frameworks. Best viewed as a web of relationships, the most common and significant categories are bureaucratic, legal, political, and professional, with the latter two types permitting greater discretion than the first two (Romzek 2000; Romzek & Dubnick 1998; Schwartz & Sulitzeanu-Kenan 2004; Thomas 1998). Bureaucratic accountability conforms to popular conceptions, including standard operating procedures and supervision for compliance with directives, rules, and regulations. Under this system, priority is given to the expectations of supervisors and other top officials and the worker is afforded little discretion (Romzek & Dubnick 1998). Maintenance of this system involves an organized and legitimate relationship between a superior and a subordinate: The need to follow orders is unquestioned, as is adherence to standard operating procedures. Expectations are managed through a hierarchical arrangement based on supervisory relationships.

Complications arise in real-world practice. The notion of public administration as a vast, finely graded hierarchy of individuals with clearly distinguished, precisely specified duties has become less popular while flattened hierarchies and collaborative networks have become more frequent. To achieve more efficient, citizen-friendly service, efforts focus on creating more complex structures that devolve authority to the lowest level, reducing the number of supervisory layers and recognizing and encouraging more diverse relationships (Stone 1995).

Under statutory accountability relationships, administrators are obligated to carry out tasks in accordance with constitutional principles, laws, and contractual obligations. The emphasis is on oversight and monitoring by authorities external to their organization to ascertain whether the obligations have been met (Romzek & Dubnick 1998). In contrast to bureaucratic accountability, legal accountability is based on relationships between a controlling party outside the agency (who is in a position to impose legal sanctions or assert formal contractual obligations) and members of the organization (Romzek & Dubnick 1987). This system manages agency expectations through a contractual relationship.

Political accountability is central to the democratic pressures imposed on public administrators. Under political accountability systems, responsiveness takes priority. The key relationship resembles that between a representative, in this case, first responders, and their constituents, those to whom they are accountable. The primary question becomes, whom does the public servant represent? Emphasis is placed on workers' exercising discretion as they face various expectations from key external groups, with a particular focus on citizen satisfaction. This system promotes responsiveness to constituents as the central tenet for managing multiple, often conflicting, expectations.

Professional accountability is characterized by placing control over organizational activities in the hands of the employee who has the expertise to get the job done. Reliance on professionals occurs with greater frequency as governments deal increasingly with technically difficult and complex problems. Public officials must rely on expertly skilled employees to provide appropriate solutions. Those employees expect to be held fully accountable for their actions and insist that agency leaders trust them to do the best job possible. The key to this system is deference to expertise within the agency (Romzek & Dubnick 1987). As such, these relationships are characterized by a high degree of autonomy and emphasize individual responsibility as the professional exercises discretion. This discretion is exercised not only about which laws, rules, or procedures are applied or enforced, but also about the nature and quality of the services delivered (Handler 1986). The assumption is that workers granted such discretion will monitor and regulate themselves through adherence to professional norms of appropriate practice (Romzek & Dubnick 1998).

With multiple masters, lines of accountability become blurred as workers find themselves facing more than one set of legitimate expectations at once. This complexity is exemplified in the work of a county chief medical examiner:

> First of all I'm accountable to myself but I'm also accountable to my colleagues here. I'm accountable to the government leadership. I'm accountable to the regulatory commission that oversees our service delivery. . . . And we're accountable to the citizens of the community here. We're accountable to them not only in how we spend their money but on the quality of the service that we provide to them.

Barbara Romzek captures these sentiments (2000, p. 40): "Like actors in repertoire theater, public administrators must be able to play a variety of roles: as obedient subordinate, innovative expert, responsive servant, and principled agent. Successful public employees stand ready to play each role as the performance expectations of the various audiences change."

Playing these roles becomes further complicated by two other elements of accountability: *accountability to* various parties and *accountability for* processes and results. "This distinction is worth making, particularly as we move beyond the two-person principal-agent case to accountability to relationships that have a complex internal structure" (Bardach & Lesser 1996, p. 200). One characteristic of front-line service providers is a tendency to regard themselves as accountable to their peers, rather than to the institutionalized system through which political, legal, and bureaucratic accountability flow (Day & Klein 1987). First response is typically a collaborative effort, and peers and partner agencies become accountable to one another for performance (Bardach & Lesser 1996). For better or worse, fellow responders exert powerful influence over each other's behavior, and peer influence often trumps supervisory control. Strong cultural bonds, "caste membership" based on rank and experience (Maynard-Moody & Musheno 2000, p. 353), and "emotion culture" (Shields & Koster 1989, p. 44) shape their beliefs, judgments, and shared group norms. A fire chief illustrates the point:

> You're accountable to your peers. I mean there's tremendous peer pressure to do the right thing: If you don't do well on a call, I think the thing that fixes it the fastest is the peer pressure.

Beyond peer accountability, there is accountability to oneself and to one's conscience. Accountability becomes a relative term when applied to emergency response and rescue. As noted above, the critical aspect of this work is the fact that the responder's life may be on the line. Police officers and firefighters accept mortal risks as part of their jobs (Nagel 1991). In the heat of a call, this constant changes the dynamic of what it means to be "accountable." A fire/air rescue captain provides an illustration:

My primary responsibility is deciding whether or not, to what extent we're going to risk ourselves . . . sometimes it can be an extremely tough call because you may be riding on someone else's chance of survival in order to ensure your own.

To Citizens

> *My responsibilities are to the public . . . we serve the public to the best of our abilities, you know? There are people who don't think that we're doing what they think we should be doing, but that's what we do.*
> —Fire Rescue Domestic Preparedness Division Chief

Interviews with first responders reveal that accountability relationships are understood to be bilateral. They recognize that they are accountable "upward" to their bureaucratic and political masters at the same time as they acknowledge they are accountable "downward" to the firefighters riding the truck and to the residents and citizens whom they assist. An officer in an urban search-and-rescue team told us on his return from deployment in Haiti that "the chain of command gets very long" and includes all levels of government and multiple jurisdictional, domestic, and international agencies. Other first responders speak about soft resources (first responders) and hard assets (tools and equipment), understanding that both are finite and that hierarchical accountability must be respected. But it is the downward accountability relationships that motivate responders whom we interviewed. Their common refrain is that their duty is to the citizens.

The distinction between state-agents and citizen-agents and the accountability relationships that attach to each provide a window into how responders perform their work. Using their interpretation of rules and procedures to guide judgments about who gets what, some front-line workers make moral judgments about the citizen-client first and then use rules, laws, and procedures to help those they consider worthy (Maynard-Moody & Musheno 2000, p. 351). Responders acknowledge that they work for the public and see justice as their duty. They describe their decisions as normative, an exercise in moral reasoning, rather than rule following or even rule breaking.

Accountability has been closely associated with the idea of "giving an account" of—that is, explaining or justifying—one's actions. It also has an alternative premise of "taking into account" the consequences of one's actions for the welfare of others. This less-developed understanding encompasses a broad range of means through which the welfare of others can be incorporated in decision making (Stone 1995). A police department public information officer provides an illustration:

A law enforcement officer on a day-to-day basis exercises more power than the president of the United States. At the stroke of a pen, at the end of a decision, I can do things in a person's life that's going to forever change it . . . [I can] decide what jobs they're going to get, but it's bigger than that because it's a ripple. Father can't get a good job because I put him in jail. Kids may not go to college, so on and so on and so on.

We now turn to how first responders enact the citizen-agent approach while being held accountable by the state.

To Agency Rules: Not-So-Standard Operating Procedures

> *It's always just a matter of the risk versus benefit and what options do we have and how are we going to make it work. Do you learn to take different skills and use them in a way different from how you've been taught? Yes. You have to, because they can't teach you for every single call that's out there. It's just impossible, so you definitely have to be able to improvise and adapt and sometimes you have to take a step back and slow things down and reassess and figure out what you've got and how you can make it work.*
> —Fire Air Rescue Captain

The jobs of first responders are inherently discretionary. The decisions they make directly affect the distribution of government goods and services and complicate accountability relationships (Kelly 1994, p. 120). The defining characteristic of first-response work is that the needs of citizens exist in tension with the demands and limits of rules (Maynard-Moody & Musheno 2000, p. 349). As Maynard-Moody and Musheno note, the street-level workers' frame of reference is not the agency or the state but the citizen encounter. They define their discretion not in terms of following, bending, or ignoring rules but as pragmatic *improvisations* in response to these encounters (pp. 349–350). Simply stated, first-response work is "rule saturated but not rule bound" (p. 336). Nearly every aspect of this work is defined by rules and procedures, yet agency rules provide only weak constraints on, and loose parameters around, judgments on the ground. Rules and procedures can never universally fit each individual and every circumstance, so judgments must be made. Discretion is a source of creativity and responsiveness; "rules of thumb" become a substitute for agency rules (Harmon & Mayer 1986, p. 334): "Without street-level discretion to interpret rules, procedures, and laws to fit the individual case, the administrative state would collapse under the weight of its own rigidity, and street-level workers would be reduced to the 'mindless technocratic functionaries' so feared by critics of bureaucracy."

Responders' relationships with citizens are personal and emotional; rarely are they cold and rational. Relationships depend largely on the category of crisis responder with whom the citizen interacts. In the event of a fire or medical emergency, firefighters and EMTs are immediately perceived by the citizenry as the "good guys." Every single time. Firefighters and EMTs do not have to figure out what happened or who is the victim. They are sworn officers who take a vow to protect and serve the public. As we saw earlier, taking an oath extends beyond the political boundaries of the jurisdiction that they formally serve. EMTs on vacation, for instance, have been known to save lives of strangers even though they are not formally on the clock or even in their jurisdiction of employment. Their jurisdiction of employment has laws on the books for the protection and safety of its citizens; firefighters and EMTs embody and implement those laws.

Police officers are also sworn officers whose authority is codified in the laws of the jurisdiction in which they are employed. A crucial difference, however, is that police officers also enforce those laws. One example of how these two groups of crisis responders and the law intersect is on the scene of, say, a fire incident. Firefighters, paramedics, and EMTs are on the scene doing their jobs—implementing the laws designed to protect and serve the citizenry as part of the harbor of refuge—and often police officers are on the scene to enforce those laws. Crowds often gather to see what is happening in a fire or medical emergency. Every morning and afternoon, we hear on the traffic reports of "gapers' delays" caused by people slowing down on the highway to check out a particularly nasty car crash. Sometimes police officers need to be there to keep crowds from interfering with firefighters' and EMTs' work, or to direct traffic away from the scene of an auto accident, likewise to let the others do their work. This is an example of different groups of responders and their relationships to the law. The firefighters and EMTs are doing their jobs and therefore upholding the law, while the police officer both upholds and enforces it. Sometimes police officers are resented for enforcing the law. This is a fundamental difference between these types of crisis responders and how they act toward the citizenry.

Police officers are not always embraced as the "good guys" when they respond to a call. Firefighters and EMTs do not confront such decisions because it is not up to them to decide who is at fault. Moreover, fire incidents and medical emergencies can be—and often are—the result of natural phenomena. Firefighters need not "blame" the lightning bolt that struck a house any more than EMTs "blame" old age for a victim's heart attack. They do not need to "do" anything about it at least. And there is usually no question who is the victim and who is not. Police officers lack such clarity, and the distrust that has arisen between law enforcement and the citizenry—no police jurisdiction "starts over," relationships are negotiated in the context of history—shapes relationships that actually get in the way of policing. Like the social worker in charge of distributing benefits, the police officer must consider whether alleged victims are "gaming the system" and trying to use the law to their own benefit. Call the cops on that neighbor you don't like; file a restraining order against an old girlfriend; get the law to intervene in your problems for you. These are the contexts within which various types of first responders must interact with the citizenry.

It is the face-to-face contact with the recipients of services coupled with geographic distance from the police department or fire station or office that weakens the link between responders and supervisors, limits the reach of rules, and makes discretion inevitable (Lipsky 1983). Stories from first responders are replete with examples of creative discretion. Below, a police officer describes a call whose success turned on an experienced officer's skill in taking an unorthodox approach:

> This person that we were dealing with was mentally ill. . . . She was on medication, so voices were speaking to her . . . I didn't know what to do. The senior police officer on the scene . . . there was a sort of a transformation in him . . . suddenly he realized that in his conversation with her that part of what she needed was a word from her priest, and so he became her priest. I'm talking about even to the point of she and he standing there with bowed heads praying.

There is nothing "standard" about the situational awareness that causes a police officer to take on the persona of a priest during an arrest. While this example shows the flip side of the image of a "mindless technocratic functionary," it renders accountability to agency rules irrelevant. To wit: "What is puzzling is that after years of disaster research on organizational behavior in major emergencies, local government continues to be surprised when their standard operating procedures in their lengthy, detailed response plans are found irrelevant in the disaster event" (Waugh 1988, p. 127).

De-emphasizing the formal, contractual relationship facilitates the "bending of rules" needed to obtain resources and to get things done during an emergency (Lewis 1988, p. 178). This is corroborated by examples of first responders getting around the system and breaking the rules in order to do their jobs. This is not to say that rules and procedures serve no function. Many of our respondents discuss standard operating procedures as guidelines or benchmarks for accountability. Training that focuses on common elements across a range of different incidents provides general tactical principles and protocols. For example, the mnemonic CRISIS serves as a memory aid for these principles and provides a flexible framework within which decisions can be made using a common, shared, and understood response language (Crichton, Flin, & Rattray 2000, pp. 213–214):

- C: Containment
- R: Resources
- I: Initiative
- S: Surprise
- I: Intelligence, and
- S: Security

Some form of this approach is utilized by many first-response agencies as standard operating guidelines. For example, a flight medic describes her script:

> You go on scene when it's raw, when everything just happened and you're basically walking in on somebody's nightmare, you know? And your own. . . . There's always an algorithm to everywhere you go. Now everything's different and you have to be flexible, but there's always going to be that same algorithm, and if you keep your mind simple . . . so I just try to not get too complex . . . I try to maintain that little algorithm. . . . Algorithm is—it's like airway, breathing, A, B, C, D, E, F, G, you know. It's like a column, an order, of things.

But standard operating guidelines go only so far. As one of our respondents stated, "What's standard about an emergency?" By definition, accountability to agency rules and the exercise of discretion are incompatible. Whether one views discretion as an "unavoidable evil" in the traditional bureaucratic sense or as a "necessary good" in practice, it is synonymous with first response (Kelly 1994, p. 139). Strict adherence to standard operating procedures is likely to be dysfunctional. Given the uniqueness of emergency situations, a prescribed set of routines to follow would exacerbate rather than solve the problem (Comfort 1988). Laws, plans, and chains of command provide crucial guidance, but none are so unambiguous that there is no room for interpretation (Stivers 2007).

After Hurricane Katrina, stories of workers refusing to bend or step outside the rules, or indeed to act at all, were legion (Stivers 2007). These sworn officers and other administrative public servants failed to uphold the spirit of the oaths they had taken. After Katrina, there was a failure to step outside the rules and act to save lives and to help those in dire need. Many decided "to renounce the exercise of discretion in favor of adhering to the letter of the law" (Stivers 2007, p. 49), to adhere strictly to bureaucratic rules and to toe the line rather than do all they could. There was a widespread "default to literalness" (Moltoch 2006, p. 32).

The decision to default to literalness breached ethical and moral commitments of some first responders after Hurricane Katrina. Neither literalness nor discretion should be characterized in such stark terms, just as the abuse of authority by some police officers cannot characterize all law enforcement. But it is important to understand that discretion and ethical behavior are not at odds. What might a "default to discretion" look like and how is it expressed outside the rules? We agree with Maynard-Moody and Leland (2000) that exercising one's professional judgment can conflict with rules. But discretion is both inevitable and desirable. It is like putty; it can be squeezed by oversight and rules but never eliminated; it will shift and reemerge in some other form in some other place (Maynard-Moody & Musheno 2000). The important thing is to take steps to ensure proper use of discretion. Many of our first responders would agree. A fire rescue captain provides a chilling example:

> I was the initial person on scene and it was pretty grotesque and it was multiple victims and I felt this need to help and to dive in. . . . The hardest thing to do as a leader is that you're not supposed to do that . . . you're supposed to assess the scene, you're supposed to determine what resources you need, you're supposed to take command. But it was so psychologically overwhelming for me . . . it was a truck that rolled over the guy . . . and it basically tore off the side of his face. It was almost like the *Terminator* movie with just all skeleton and just an eyeball so it was that grotesque and that magnetic that you just couldn't pull yourself from it. . . . When somebody's screaming for your help and they're grabbing their face like this, that it's hard not to do anything; when you're a commander and you're in charge of the scene and you told people to do it and you have somebody who's a rookie and they can't help this guy, how do you *not* [help] when you know you can?

One of his colleagues provides an example of exercising judgment by breaking the rules when the safety of the crew is on the line:

> There were three people shot. We were told on the dispatch that police have arrived and it's okay to come in, and when we get there, there's a riot scene pretty much. So it wasn't safe for us to come in yet. I have two severely critical patients and one who's not critical but is shot . . . by the

rule I should be taking only one . . . but what I judged was an unsafe scene. I broke the rules, and I took both of them and . . . they weren't packaged correctly. We left the riot scene, parked to the side of the road and . . . fixed the patients and packaged them correctly, but at that moment I broke all the rules for the safety of my guys . . . I saw an unsafe scene and my guys are working on an unsafe scene where people are yelling at us and throwing rocks at us and stuff like that and I said, hey, throw them both in the truck. Let's get out of here.

Decision making in such a situation is not a cool intellectual process. It occurs in the midst of hot emotional reactions. Nagel suggests that when decision makers are faced with an emotionally consequential, no-win choice, how they cope with the problem depends on two factors: hope and time. If decision makers see realistic hope of finding a solution superior to any of the risky options that are immediately apparent, then their efforts are likely to follow a pattern that Janis and Mann (1977) call *vigilance*, which is close kin to the rational-comprehensive ideal (Nagel 1991). If, however, decision makers lose hope of an acceptable option, they are likely to fall into either of two patterns of defective decision processes: namely, *defensive avoidance*—involving procrastination—or *hypervigilance*—involving too much emotional arousal and too much haste, but no true vigilance (Janis & Mann 1977).

The tension between accountability to agency rules and exercising discretion is also viewed from the perspective of emotional adaptability. People who maintain an other-oriented disposition toward the expression of emotion are more willing and able to adapt their emotional expression to the social environment (Schaubroeck & Jones 2000). Hochschild refers to this as an ability to develop a "healthy false self" in which "inauthentic" emotions are readily expressed in service of the role (1983, p. 195). This trait is known as emotional adaptability, which is the ability to alter one's usual response in order to meet the demands of the job. A fire/air rescue flight medic provides an illustration:

Why isn't this happening the way it should? What do we need to fix in order to make it smooth? So you just have to be creative . . . we didn't have the correct thing to [secure the airway] so we made up something else. . . . So my process is why isn't it coming out smooth and find out why and then fix it and that's what the pause is for . . . some [calls] are ugly like they were meant to not be smooth but everybody stayed calm and adapted to whatever situation came, and it just went smoothly.

Taken together, this web of accountability relationships, bureaucratic and legal (agency rules), political (citizens), and professional (peers), as well as accountability to oneself, complicates the work of first responders. They attempt to simplify it by focusing on the performance of their public duty. The bottom line is to help the greatest number of people with the least risk to others. They rationalize and justify their decisions as necessary. Whether first responders learn how to reconcile conflicting accountabilities on the job, or whether they sidestep the attempt, is explored next.

How Workers Reconcile Conflicting Accountabilities

How do workers reconcile conflicting accountabilities? The short answer to this question is, they may not. A profound sense of duty, pragmatism, and the exigencies of the moment can override attention to how to reconcile conflicting accountabilities. The exercise of discretion and the moral and value judgments that accompany it may render the goal of reconciliation misplaced, even irrelevant. While first responders are bound by a long tether of accountability relationships, discretion permeates every decision and every action (Maynard-Moody & Musheno 2000). Workers operate in a context established by law and organizational rules, but they interpret what these influences mean in specific cases (Vinzant & Crothers 1998).

Experienced decision makers develop a capacity for professional judgment that demonstrates a significant amount of creativity. In practice, they form judgments based upon incomplete, often conflicting information that is guided by a set of professional standards and a disciplined body of knowledge (Comfort 1988). By substituting their pragmatic judgments for the unrealistic and untenable views of those with formal authority, the street-level workers are, in their own view, acting responsibly. They assume the burden of making moral and pragmatic judgments that alter the lives of citizens (Maynard-Moody & Musheno 2000). As such, rather than seeking to reconcile competing accountabilities, first responders aspire first and foremost to save lives and property. If they are called to account, many of our respondents told us they would rather ask forgiveness than permission.

As we examine below, measuring accountability in the dynamic environment of crisis response is as much art as it is science. Dror (1988, p. 261) refers to decision making under disaster conditions as "fuzzy gambling" in the sense that decisions must be made in the face of uncertainty, and the rules of the gamble are largely unknowable, often indeterminate, and usually erratic. Decision making under these conditions is a haphazard process and is likely to be error prone because of inherent difficulties and limitations. "This conclusion is important for the evaluation of [decision making under disaster conditions] and for application of various political and legal forms of accountability to it" (1988, p. 263). We turn now to the emotive skills that are inherent in the work of first responders and emergency services personnel.

Emotive Skills

The essential skill of emotional labor is managing one's own emotions and attempting to manage the emotions of another in order to do one's job. One of the conclusions we have drawn from our prior research is that these higher-order emotive skills are most conspicuous when they are absent. Our current research validates earlier findings and extends our understanding of emotive work as it is applied in emergency, crisis, and disaster response. The skills required to manage one's emotions as the "face" of government in crisis situations are even more diverse and multi-dimensional than we expected.

What does it take to develop a state of "pseudocalm" when working on the edge of chaos (Janis & Mann 1977, p. 85) in order to suppress troubling thoughts and avoid painful memories (Nagel 1991)? What brings a police captain to calm an offender by assuming the persona of a priest in order to make a safe arrest? Discretion is at the heart of first-response work, and creative emotive skills are essential. Creativity has long been considered an essential component of the emergency management process because emergency conditions pose ill-structured problems that defy prior expectations for action (Comfort 1989).

We examine these creative emotive skills that responders utilize on the job, specifically the mental pictures they develop as they size up a situation. As professionals trained to serve and protect, first responders are expected to maintain a poised presence even under the most tragic of circumstances. As Pogrebin and Poole (1991, p. 397) observe of police officers,

> in the face of human tragedy, officers must maintain their composure, distancing themselves from intense emotional reactions evoked in such encounters. Police generally believe that the public expects them to be fearless and calm, able to handle critical situations in an objective manner. The standards that police set for themselves for managing emotions are often severe and uncompromising.

During our interviews, many responders described situations in which they attempted to inhibit outward signs of emotion. Richards and Gross (1999) refer to inhibiting overt emotion-expressive behavior as emotion suppression, a cognitively demanding form of self-regulation. Successful emotion suppression is thought to require an internal dialogue in which individuals must remind themselves to suppress, self-monitor for signs of unwanted emotional impulses, and evaluate how well they are doing (1999). One way to control and suppress one's emotions on the job is to attempt to depersonalize the work. A chief medical examiner explains:

I have on occasion done autopsies on police officers that I've worked with that have died in the line of duty. . . . Dealing with the tragedy of the situation comes with time; it almost becomes automatic where you clearly are looking at it from a scientific basis and the humanness and the person connected to those particular remains, you automatically divorce yourself from. . . . You separate yourself from the component of it though, so it is an exercise in gathering information and interpretation of the scientific and medical evidence. You just have to get past the human side.

A fire-rescue chief operates from a similar approach:

We had a news camera crew riding with us. They were looking at developing this TV show about paramedics, and we had a call where this car had crossed the center line and hit directly head on into another vehicle. . . . It was a very bad accident. The mother that I was taking care of was in terrible shape and pinned in the car . . . we worked for probably forty-five minutes to cut her out of the car to get her to the hospital, and after the call I look over and the camera man has his head in his hands, he had just thrown up, he was wrecked and he said he had never seen anything like that and he doesn't know how we even deal with that. . . . We got back to the station and he put the video in to show us what he had shot . . . and it hit me. I realized it. I mean he was focusing in. I couldn't even tell you what that woman looked like. I never personalize it—I never put a face with the person. I think we just block everything out . . . and it hit me, he personalized it. He was zooming in on her face, on my face . . . he was making it much more personal and I think we separate ourselves from that. . . . You've created such a block.

While experienced first responders learn to depersonalize their work during a call, personal reflection and critical incident debriefing come into play after the call. A fire/air rescue captain talks about how she functions on the job:

You kind of go into autopilot and for instance on that call itself there really weren't any emotions that I noticed. It's not until afterwards when you stop acting that you start reflecting on what happened that you start to feel those kinds of things.

Dealing with death and human tragedy on a daily basis can shake even the most experienced worker. First-response work becomes a cumulative experience with unanticipated consequences. Here a fire chief describes a call:

We have a raging house fire that we're storming into . . . we are crawling through this house and we're in the area where there's the heaviest fire, and I'm sitting on something and I reach between my legs and I shine the light and it's the victim, burnt real, you know, dead . . . turned out there were four kids and a mother that lost her job and decided she can't deal with it anymore and she burned up herself and the whole house . . . and I couldn't get past this thing, I mean it rocked my world, you know? I think more than ever now you don't know which one is going to catch you. I've been in hundreds of fires, I've found hundreds of victims, you never know which one is going to get you and that one just rocked my world.

Emotive skills are manifest in managing conflict and relationships. These skills are inherent in the work of first responders:

You spend most of your time as a police officer—we call ourselves mobile counselors really—you spend most of your time as a police officer trying to help people that aren't getting along well be more civil and get along; resolve their conflicts without hurting each other or resorting to violence or some other crime.

The emotional component to crisis response takes many forms. It can be maintaining a connection with a victim's family, as the following vignette illustrates:

He runs over to the kid that he hit and fires several rounds from a gun into this kid and kills him. The kid dies behind the wheel. His mother has no husband, that's her only child, she loves her son, wonderful, wonderful, wonderful relationship. She is forever brokenhearted, so much so that she basically dies in misery a few years later and would often call me out of the blue and just cry on the phone. Sometimes I'd take her out to lunch just to try to give her some connection because she saw me as a lifeline, as a homicide detective working that case, she saw me sort of as a lifeline or the last line to her son.

Handler (1986, p. 18) suggests that "dependent people—poor, minorities, the uneducated, unsophisticated—are often at a serious disadvantage [in their relationships with street-level workers]. They lack the information, skills, and the power to persuade. The official has the unfair advantage." Citizen-clients must yield to street-level workers to receive state benefits or to avoid state sanctions; they must follow orders (Maynard-Moody & Musheno 2000). But citizen-clients, even if they are not legal citizens, can minimize any disadvantage by resorting to different ploys. A confounding dynamic in communicating with people in distress or desperation is the experience of being manipulated. Skillful listening comes into play when attempting to discern fact from fiction. A chief in the U.S. Coast Guard talks about these high-stakes mind games:

> If you're doing migrant operations . . . they game play. . . . There was this one woman who had convinced this doctor that she was deathly sick and then they said, okay, we'll put you in the helicopter and we're taking you to Nassau. Nassau? she said. I want to go to Miami. We said no, we're taking you to Nassau. And all of a sudden she was healed. So that's the game you end up playing.

What emotive skills come into play as responders arrive on the scene of a call? We examine these processes next.

The Size-Up: Taking a Mental Picture

Emotive skills are key to grasping the scope of a call and deciding upon a course of action that will determine the outcome. First responders need to make quick decisions in complex, dynamic, and hazardous situations, with limited time and information (Brunacini 1985; Crichton et al. 2000). The U.S. Armed Forces developed a training technique called Tactical Decision Games (TDGs) to improve tactical skill and decision-making ability (Schmitt 1994). TDGs foster the development of shared or compatible mental models of the task and the roles of each participant, and skills such as situation awareness and leadership (Crichton et al. 2000). Regular repetition of calls leads to the development of a significant mental experience bank whereby decision making at the start of actual incidents becomes intuitive based on recognition of development patterns. First responders rely upon a similar process. Accumulated successes and failures, in work and in personal life, form a set of experiences on which they draw in particular situations. Intuition resembles a mental map generated from years of practice (Burke & Miller 1999). A police captain provides an illustration:

> You are it. And so you draw from a pool of all your life experiences, all your training, all of your education, all of those things, and all of them that you have, I think, the better and more successful you are in the profession, but you have to have a mental bag of tricks that come for all those things when you go on a scene and you know it's rather than just rapid fire, it's rapid thought.

This experiential database is fundamental to the "size-up" of a call scene.

> I'm forced to take a mental picture for an instant and transpose that mental picture into the next action, whatever it may be. The term that's used is size-up.

This mental process begins en route to the call as the team leader senses his physiologic response to lights and sirens. Calming himself by focusing on his breathing and voice modulation helps him appear and sound calm as he talks to other responders on the radio. Simultaneously, a mental picture of what he is about to see is forming. Mental pictures may develop from an intangible sixth sense that can come into play on the scene, as we discuss next.

Experience and the Intangible Sixth Sense

Crisis response is as much art as science. Experienced responders quickly and accurately achieve situation awareness, based on their awareness of patterns, their ability to make fine discriminations between cues, and their familiarity with prototypical cases. These qualities permit them to detect anomalies (Crichton et al. 2000). Interviews with fire and police personnel were replete with examples of these skills. A fire rescue chief explains:

> You know, I can't put my finger on it . . . sometimes we don't catch everything and people don't do well as a result because we didn't catch everything, but you learn from that. I've missed a victim in a house and there were certain things I remember that I never forgot, and fifteen years later I ended up finding a victim and a couple of other people had missed him and they said how did you find him and certain things, I heard water running and the person had sought refuge in the shower and I had remembered that from fifteen years ago, saying I'm never going to forget again that sound of the running water, and I ended up going into the bathroom where they weren't supposed to be and they were right there in the bathtub.

An example from a police lieutenant is equally insightful:

> A great deal of the job is acting. You're constantly acting, you're constantly improvising on a scene and adapting to the situation . . . from scene to scene, from incident to incident you're adapting, adjusting.

The lieutenant's words amplify reality: Acting and improvising do not lend themselves to measurement. This is why the work is as much art as science.

Measuring Accountability: A Moving Target

> *One of the things I tell the kids in the police academy is that most*
> *times you get a fifty percent favorability rating. If you arrest a rob-*
> *ber, his mother is not happy with you. The victim's mother thinks*
> *that you're a hero.*
>
> —Police Captain

In public service parlance, "accountability for" is invariably followed by the word "results." But what results, and how do we know when they have been achieved? Bardach and Lesser (1996) view accountability for results as shorthand. It is a way of saying that it is accountability for a better quality of effort directed toward the results being measured. Such effort includes accountability for choosing priorities wisely and making choices about which services to deliver to whom. A trauma center doctor illustrates:

> We had a case, you may have heard it on the news. The Italian family that was here getting hyperbaric treatment for their son with cerebral palsy and the hyperbaric chamber caught fire. And the grandmother was in the chamber with the child and both were severely burned. That is a very challenging situation. Now we have a language barrier, you're trying to call another country, locate a parent to notify them about the situation . . . here we had a seven-, eight-year-old child who went through a very severe injury and all of the physicians worked on the child so that left no one for the grandmother so the grandmother did expire because of a decision that all four surgeons would work to save this child at once. And nobody questions that decision. They still feel that it was the best to do because the child is the more salvageable individual.

Accountability, like merit, may be in the eye of the beholder: One person's favorable assessment may be another's criticism. The following quote by a chief of fire rescue starkly illustrates this point:

> We had a six- or seven-year-old girl who was hit by a car and run over, had tire tracks on her chest and back, and we're working on her in the back of the truck and we're trying to intubate her, couldn't get her intubated properly, went into the esophagus. We found out later on the girl died eventually and we were actually second-guessed by the people at the hospital: "You didn't put the tube in properly and the IV was this and that." I went ballistic on them basically and I wrote a nice, long letter to them: "I challenge *any* of you to come out and work in a moving closet with six people trying to attend to a six-year-old with minimal lighting going corners at forty miles per hour trying to save the girl's life."

Measuring accountability is problematic also in terms of verification. This refers to problems in the measures and means for ascertaining whether one's performance expectations have been met (Romzek & Dubnick 1998). Another dimension to measuring accountability is the problem of "many hands" (Thompson 1982). Many social and regulatory programs are implemented through an elaborate array of intergovernmental arrangements, and the delegation of authority for particular government programs is often dispersed across a number of agencies, all of whom are collaborating (Romzek & Dubnick 1998). This process is characteristic of much of the work of crisis and emergency response. The World Trade Center disaster of September 11, 2001, is a case in point. A disaster response system of nearly 500 public, private, and nonprofit organizations engaged in response operations during the first three weeks (Comfort 2002). Other sources identified more than 1,400 nonprofit organizations involved in recovery activities over a six-month period (Kapucu 2003). A retired operations chief for the U.S. Coast Guard and a regional Homeland Security Task Force provides another illustration:

> [In the case of human smuggling] it's unfathomable sometimes why they would [turn against a family member] . . . but I would suspect that they're threatened . . . you kinda get led astray . . . when somebody's trying to confuse you and a life or lives are in jeopardy you really have to move quickly. So a lot of times what'll happen is that the . . . Coast Guard, Border Patrol and others, ICE, the Immigration and Customs Enforcement will get the local Miami police department, Broward Sheriff, whoever, to knock on the door and try and help piece together what's going on.

The tension that exists between competing definitions of success poses another problem for measuring accountability. First responders can decide to make their work harder, more dangerous, and less officially "successful" in order to respond to the needs of the individual. They can overinvest their time and the state's resources even though the chance of success is slim (Maynard-Moody & Musheno 2000, 2003). A U.S. Coast Guard officer tells of keeping a case open long after it could have been reasonably closed:

> The hardest thing to assess is someone's will to live. . . . We had a Dominican fishing boat sink at night off the coast of the Dominican Republic the year before—twenty fishermen go in the water. We looked for a couple of days and found maybe half of them. . . . We were well past what the tables said that they could survive. . . . You know a friend of mine said Dominicans are tough people. You know, they're gonna keep swimming, so we kept looking. We went twice as long as the tables said they could survive . . . found one guy four days later, swimming the whole time.

As a final point, we turn now to the relationship between accountability and expectations on the job.

Managing Expectations

> *You have to be cognizant of where you're at, who you are, what socioeconomic environment you're in and how they [recipients of service] really perceive you. If I work in the ghetto . . . and they look at you [as someone who is] going to take care of them and you're going to help them. . . . They need you to help them . . . if you treat them properly and correctly, they'll look at you [positively]. Whereas if you go to Aventura [an affluent neighborhood], she's having a heart attack . . . and the guy nearly threw a fit because the "servant" got blood on the comforter, so it's the inverse. They'll look at you more as a servant, not somebody to take care of you. So if you're not aware of what environment you're in, then you're not really trying to understand where the patient's coming from.*
>
> —Fire Rescue Captain

Governmental accountability is broader than the traditional narrow association of accountability with answerability. Rather, it involves the various "means by which public agencies and their workers manage the diverse expectations generated within and outside the organization" (Romzek & Dubnick 1987, p. 228). In these terms, accountability may be defined as the satisfaction of legitimate expectations about the use of administrative discretion, or the legitimization of discretion (Stone 1995).

Dealing with expectations is central to the work of public administration (Dubnick & Romzek 1993). One type is the role expectations that citizens have for the agency. Another is public servants' awareness of workplace culture and how their emotional labor strategies are (or are not) tailored to address cultural contingencies of the workplace (situational emotional labor). Both these types, external plus internal, combine to inform our understanding of how crisis responders function on the job. Dubnick and Romzek (ibid.) suggest that public administrators behave in a manner that is driven by the need to effectively cope with expectations. This perspective leads us to yet another way of viewing accountability systems. It is a means through which public administrators, including first responders, seek to manage multiple, diverse, interactive, and often contradictory expectations. Dubnick and Romzek identify a number of factors that shape public administration expectations, including intensity, temporality (time-based), tractability (relating to "impossible jobs"), and interrelatedness. Simon (1997, p. 359) regards expectations as a central characteristic of "purposive" group behavior:

A's decision may depend on his expectation of B's behavior, while B's decision may depend on his expectation of A's behavior . . . the expectations of these participants will be a factor in determining their behavior. . . . In this sense administration is not unlike play-acting. The task for the good actor is to know and play his role, although different roles may differ greatly in content.

Crisis response is a team endeavor. For our respondents, their modus operandi is to work collaboratively as a well-functioning team. The safety and success of each call depends upon "accurate expectations as to what the others are going to do" (Simon 1997, p. 81). In other words, safety and success depend on complementarities of expectations (Parsons & Shils 1951).

Met or unmet expectations can be explained in terms of the "gap" between what governments are prepared to do in emergency management situations (i.e., bureaucratic norms) and what emerges as the expectations of those victimized by the disaster (i.e., emergent norms that guide social interactions). According to Schneider, "the gap is the primary determinant of public perceptions about the success or failure of governmental relief efforts" (Schneider 1992, p. 135). Government is the provider of last resort. Denial of service is not an option, even when demand for services far exceeds the capacity to respond. Expectations can be based and compounded on past experiences that cue emotional recall. A fire-rescue captain explains:

> In instances where we are dealing with a family tragedy where emotions are high, where there perhaps has already been a past experience with the fire department that has molded the opinion of that family . . . I may have never dealt with that family before, but clearly someone in a uniform in my department has, and they took that experience and harbored it and are enacting it upon my crew when I get there, so I have to understand that by simply trying to do the best that I can, stepping back, quieting down, understanding that they're going through a horrific time possibly at this moment and I just walked into a circumstance that was probably already not on an even keel.

Summary

The nature of first response blurs and confounds the simple model of accountability assumed in textbook theories. The work is dynamic and uncertain, and determinations of performance differ by vantage point. The multiple dimensions to assessing effectiveness shape interpretations of what accountability should look like. Vignettes in this discussion use words of responders to bring into focus these practices: "how" they function on the job, their accountability relationships, and the emotive skills they use to manage them. They were more likely to emphasize informal accountability relationships (downward, horizontal, and to the community being served) than hierarchical, upward accountability. The picture that emerges, highlighting professionalism, teamwork, and adaptability in the face of indescribable human drama, gives us a fuller appreciation of what it takes to perform this work in multiple contexts—on the ground, in the air, or at sea—and how professional judgment, discretion, diverse expectations, and an abiding sense of duty shape the web of accountability relationships.

6

Of the People

Legitimacy, Representativeness, and the Difference That Gender Makes

In February 2008, Jody Weis was appointed the new superintendent of police for the Chicago Police Department (CPD). From 1985 to 2007, Weis had been a federal agent with the Federal Bureau of Investigations (FBI) in Philadelphia. Weis was a civilian when he was selected for the CPD position and only the second superintendent out of fifty-four to ever come from outside the city. He was not a police officer who came up through the ranks, and he is not allowed to wear the CPD uniform, although he did so at ceremonial events. From the perspective of the rank and file, Superintendent Weis faced legitimacy challenges and, in fact, received two "no confidence" votes in 2009 and 2010 from the Fraternal Order of Police.

This chapter says less about emotional labor per se and more about the characteristics of those who perform it. This topic matters because it relates to the legitimacy of government action. Citizens' trust in public providers is an important contributor to successful response outcomes, which makes legitimacy an important matter. It affects the level of rapport between responder and citizen. To begin, we focus on the people who perform the work in terms of their representativeness and the authority conferred upon them. From there, we drill down to the subject of gender and discuss the difference that it makes.

Legitimacy

American attitudes about government are conflicted. While one inherent value is to distrust power and want government "out of sight and out of mind," it is still the default resource when citizens are in crisis. And when they call 911 for help, they welcome governmental actors into their homes. Thus, the work

101

of first responders is the face of government that citizens like. The captain of a fire rescue operation describes it this way:

> I spend most of my time working in lower economic areas and by choice because I think that's where we make the biggest difference. . . . But that doesn't give you the right to be condescending or belittling to anybody because they will call you on it in a heartbeat, you know? They will recognize it and they will recognize it as a government coming down on them again and telling them what to do and it can quickly get out of control.

Legitimacy such as described by the captain is essential for any government-to-citizen interaction to work. It manifests itself as a matter of trust, such that when citizens seek help, first responders appear on the scene and are welcomed and are treated with deference. This allows them to go to work immediately and address whatever crisis is at hand. Says a member of a fire rescue squad:

> We see families for, at most, thirty to sixty minutes at a time, so to develop a relationship or trust is [not going to happen]. They're trusting not the individual that responds to the call. They're trusting the system and they're trusting the department as for our reputation.

Trust is essential and based not on any one-on-one relationship, but on the legitimate use of power and authority, citizens' image of governmental services, and their expectations about the competence of workers. The captain of an air rescue helicopter team notes that firefighters are one of the only groups of people whom citizens willingly let inside their house:

> When you feel sick you open your door to the paramedic—a fire rescue department—and you know that when they come in they're going to take care of you; they're going to transport you or somehow get you help. I think as a firefighter, I've never been in a situation where I've gone in to try to help somebody and they say no, no, no, don't come and help me. So I think the trust comes by reputation and word of mouth.

This trust is a two-sided coin—a double-edged sword. Responders know that they must live up to the expectations citizens have of them. The captain continues:

> When people come and they thank me for the job that I do, I look at it as I don't need to be thanked because this is what the citizens pay me for. So I find it as more of a duty for me because I'm employed in a profession

where it is required for me to act a certain way and to be trained a certain way and to perform a certain way. I figured if they call me, they assumed that I'm trained and I'm a professional and I know what I'm doing so to me it's like my job. That's the way I look at it.

These words connote understanding that there is an obligation between citizens and responders. The former must trust that help is being delivered and the latter must hold their work to a high standard such that their actions meet citizen expectations. The power of the state is best achieved when those who hold the power use it well. Another captain observes,

We're fortunate that people really love us. It sure makes our job a lot easier. But the best thing we can do to gain their trust is just be professional and be good at what we do and try to put our heart into it. I mean, we'll try to treat people like they're our own family. If you go about it in that manner, the right thing ends up happening and everybody's happy.

These quotes make it clear that responders could not do their work without the legitimacy of the state and the trust of citizens. Trust is established through belief in the competence of public services, belief that the responder has the citizen's best interests at heart, and belief that the stranger who has arrived to help them will help, not hurt, them. In other words, identification with the responder as "someone like me" is an important aspect of the credibility of responders' expertise. It is for this reason that demographic representation is important in the public workforce, whether among firefighters, law enforcement, or any other type of services.

And what of the application of discretion to frontline service providers? Can we assume, as Sowa and Selden (2003) concluded for upper-level administrators, that first responders may care more, may try harder, to save those who are like themselves? Clearly, many of those whom we interviewed talked of how important it was to save a child and, when they failed, how much harder it was for them to accept the bad outcome. What, besides a child in need, might cause squads to go above and beyond their usual performance? Does the crisis victim's demographic background, whether it is gender, race, religion, or ethnicity, lead to a powerful creation of identity in such a way that it is easier for responders to care more for those who are like themselves, as Krislov (1974) and Krislov & Rosenbloom (1981) remind us? Although no one we interviewed said that they exercised discretion in such a way as to deliver services in a discriminatory fashion, they did report their levels of unease when they found themselves responding to a call in a neighborhood that was racially or ethnically different from their own. For example, in the quote below, an EMT relates his unease when he responds to a call in a neighborhood where everyone around the victim is different from him. His uniform helps to "standardize" his appearance as an authority figure but even that, he fears, may put him at risk. In this quote, the EMT expresses his unease over his differentness and his concern that he will be at risk:

> If you walk into a situation—a shooting or a stabbing—and there's fifty people out there, I don't know who shot or stabbed this person, particularly if they are in a neighborhood where they are all from the same background and you're not, they're looking at you differently like you might represent authority that they don't want. I might be concerned that someone else might have a gun and pull it out. You have to look at all of that.

The uniform is a symbol that conveys authority, expertise, and status. In situations such as described above by the EMT, uniforms convey the power of the state and in the best of circumstances convey a message of legitimacy and competence. These attributes usually elicit deference from the citizen. Uniforms overcome demographic differences among responders and serve to standardize each person's appearance, conferring power on the wearer. Differences in decorations denote the rank and status of the wearer, providing a shorthand so that everyone responding to the call knows who is in charge. Partially amplifying the value of a uniform and partially explaining how a positive image wards off a hostile public, a chief of a fire rescue division explains how the division's work is visible and likely to be videotaped without firefighters knowing it. This constrains the usual repartee among teammates that would occur in less visible occupations. He says:

> The role of the uniform is significant in many respects, and what we try to impart upon our personnel is you are held to a higher standard than everyone else if you're wearing that uniform. The simple things, going on a big call where you haven't seen anyone for six months, a year, you have to be very careful about high fiving or "how are you doing?" or give them a hug. There's a time and place for it. But you have to understand that every call we go on is a disaster to someone and whether we put the fire out, whether the call is over, somebody is either watching on TV or somebody's looking and saying these guys were laughing while this house burned, and that may not be the case at all but that's the perception and so we tell them this. There are people out there, especially nowadays: everybody has a camera, everybody wants to take your picture, not because you're a celebrity or because they want to be your friend—they want to find something wrong with what you do. Even on an off-duty basis, if you're going to wear a T-shirt, if you

want to wear a hat that says Miami-Dade Fire Rescue, you have to act more appropriately than you would under normal circumstances.

This quote makes clear that legitimacy is tenuous, always vulnerable if citizen expectations are violated. The fact that emergency response is so visible means that responders must always be "on" when at a call. The risks associated with visibility contribute to the emotional labor demands of the job. This is because they require a greater degree of emotional suppression than would be necessary if the team could simply do its job without considering whether it will appear on YouTube tomorrow. We turn now to another aspect of representation, which is gender, and discuss how it factors into the performance of women and men in crisis response.

How Gender Affects Emotive Aspects of Crisis Response

The difference that gender makes in terms of emotional labor is, at one level, elusive and, at another level, well documented. Formal studies have found that there is not a significant difference in the way emotions are experienced by men and women (Brody 1985; Brody & Hall 2008). And there is not a difference between women's and men's ability to perform emotion work (Guy, Newman, & Mastracci 2008). However, there is a significant difference in how emotions are expressed (Birnbaum 1983; Hess et al. 2000; Simon & Nath 2004). These differences even extend to how nonverbal communication is received (Hertenstein & Keltner 2010; Hickson, Stacks, & Moore 2004; Mehrabian 2007). There is also a difference in how the performance of emotional labor affects women as compared to men, especially in regard to how they cope with intensely traumatic experiences (Kring & Gordon 1998). Below we discuss several dimensions that pertain to gender difference in the performance of emotional labor: job segregation, emotion culture, gendered expectations for emotional expressivity, and the wage penalty for men who work in emotionally intense jobs.

Job Segregation

The effect of gender conflates with job segregation to produce unique emotion cultures in the workplace. Occupations performed primarily by men have masculine work cultures, while those performed primarily by women have feminine cultures. Both types of culture have their own display rules for emotive expression. The emotion culture in a predominantly male work unit discourages overt expression of fear, lack of confidence, and sadness and discourages talk that processes intense emotional experiences. The emotion culture in predominantly female work units, on the other hand, encourages the discussion of feelings and overt processing of intense emotional experiences. In the paragraphs that follow, we discuss these differences.

Emotional labor is performed by both men and women, and there are not significant differences in their ability or competence at performing it (Guy et al. 2008; Hsieh & Guy 2009; Jin & Guy 2009). However, there are gendered expectations in terms of what kind of emotional labor is performed and how it manifests itself. Jobs that score high in terms of emotional labor demands are about evenly split between women's jobs and men's jobs. Gendered jobs—for example, police work versus social work—develop norms and display rules that create their own emotion cultures. While men's jobs tend to emphasize impassive toughness, women's emphasize communication skills. According to U.S. Census data, job segregation is such that 77 percent of correctional institution officers are male, 82 percent of police officers and detectives are male, only 30 percent of social workers are male, and only 7 percent of registered nurses are male (Bhave & Glomb 2009). The greatest consternation comes with job integration, when someone of the minority gender enters a workforce that is predominantly the other. A female firefighter talks about how it feels to be the "other":

> As a firefighter I get a lot of, "Oh, women don't belong in the fire service." That was easy for me to deal with because I knew they weren't right. I just did my job and let my actions speak for me and just brush them off because . . . at that point there's really nothing you can do, but whenever somebody questions things like that, that definitely makes you question yourself.

The last words of this quote demonstrate that being an X in a group of Os causes this firefighter to be constantly on guard, making sure that everything she does is right, knowing that she is being watched and her every action evaluated. The threat to her self-confidence may cause her to be less assertive than she otherwise might be.

Emotion Culture

There is a connection between crisis responders' efforts and culturally determined, gender-based norms of appropriate behavior. The question of interest is this: although both male and female public servants engage in emotional labor, are the *characteristics* of their efforts determined substantially by cultural norms of sex-appropriate behavior? Is there a degree to which role legitimacy interacts with job to shape how emotions are expressed? Explanations by responders help to discern the answers to these questions. When a female captain of a fire/air rescue team was interviewed about the aspects of her job that pertain to emotional support, she responded,

> There's not only the patient that needs the emotional support, the knowledge of what's going on and what's getting ready to happen to them, but there's also the family members or friends that have to be there that can't be forgotten and sometimes they're overlooked and that's a big part of it. And also sometimes it comes down to the other people that you're working with because of some of the situations that we're put in.
>
> One particular instance was about ten years ago. We responded to an accident on Christmas night on I-75. It was an SUV that had rolled over. Father, stepmother, and about a seven- or eight-year-old boy and the boy was trapped in the vehicle and lost most of his arm and we couldn't get a surgeon on scene—couldn't get the boy out of the car—had to make the decision with the permission of the surgeon that we were on the radio with to finish amputating the arm on scene so we could get the boy out and get him to the hospital. It was hard for everybody, but I had a rookie on my truck. She had only been on a few months and she had been a nurse for thirteen years but nurses are definitely not—unless they work in an ER and even then—they're not first responders. They're not used to what we see, and I ended up helping her out a lot and actually ended up—which I didn't like—I went and visited the child in the hospital afterwards with her because she needed that. She needed to go see him. So there's all kinds of emotional support that has to go on and especially with the dominantly male field. I think it's buried way too much.

Interviewer: Is it part of your training?

> No, no. Not at all. The only thing you get in terms of that is they talk about critical incident debriefing and that anybody can ask for it. But I think the problem is they wait for people to ask for it. And in this instance I had to suggest three or four times that we have a debriefing after this call before they finally had one. And it turned out that a lot of people were really affected by that call. There were a lot of tears shed because it was frustrating. It was a very frustrating call because we couldn't get the child out.

This quote is notable because it illuminates the intensity of emotion and the extra effort that the female captain expended to help the rookie resolve her feelings about the event. Whether a male captain would have engaged in the same depth of emotional labor to help the rookie deal with the leftover feelings from the call can only be left to speculation. It is also important to note the captain's statement that "there's all kinds of emotional support that has to go on and especially with the dominantly male field," which demonstrates the extra burden that women in the squad carry, and the suggestion that she resents it, "which I didn't like." This case amplifies laboratory findings that women have a deeper emotional drain from intense experiences such as this.

In fields where men predominate, the culture tends to discourage emotional expressions that pertain to weakness. And some fields, such as firefighting, are particularly difficult for women to gain access to. When those in command posts refer to a "brotherhood" in our interviews with them, it is obvious that women's involvement is an afterthought. This is said more overtly by the chief of a fire rescue domestic preparedness division:

> The unfortunate thing with the fire service is it's a macho operation—always has been, regardless of if you have females involved or not. Most males in firefighting and in public safety in general aren't going to be the first ones to tell you that there's something wrong. They don't want to let you know that they need assistance, and that's something we have to change the culture on, which is exceptionally difficult. It's changing very slowly. The makeup of the fire services has changed tremendously over the past year—used to be very white-male dominated and it's become very, very diverse, but in this particular case again you've got, "Oh I can do this, I'm fine, don't worry about me."

In this case, the chief is talking about the reluctance among firefighters to admit that a call is stressful and their tendency to deny lingering issues related to it. This reluctance causes psychic injury in the form of post-traumatic stress disorder that ultimately affects productivity when burnout results.

Gendered Expectations for Emotional Expression

Sociologists who examine emotions report that women are more likely to talk about their feelings with others, while men are more likely to use mood-altering substances. The fact that women cope with stressful experiences by seeking social support indicates that employers can more easily use team meetings and self-care plans to help them debrief and manage the flood of feelings that accompany "bad" calls. These methods do not work as well for men because they are accustomed to holding back expression of emotion (Simon & Nath 2004). Critical incident debriefings are the exception for men, while they are the rule for women. Stated differently, while debriefings must be imposed on men, women will seek them out. Another gender difference in terms of expressivity is that women express anger verbally while men express anger behaviorally. This means that maladaptive behaviors, such as fights and substance abuse, are high on the risk list for men.

Two points are clear from this discussion: First, each workplace has its own emotion culture driven by norms, expectations, and values. First responders have firmly held beliefs about when and how emotional expression is acceptable or desirable. Second, gender plays a role in that it defines the culture, whether one of silence or one of expressivity.

The police culture—a masculine culture—differs significantly from the work culture of victim assistance advocates, a feminine culture. While police are reluctant to express fear or insecurity and are loath to discuss their emotions in an open forum, the opposite is the case for victim assistance advocates. For police or firefighters, their attendance at debriefings, which are designed to help them relieve the stress from the event, may or may not be effective. It is up to the individual officer to take advantage of the opportunity. Because of the emotional conditioning of the job, coupled with early socialization experiences, debriefing is difficult for men because it contradicts years of conditioning.

In jobs that scoff at tears, it is challenging to construct training and development that will fit within the norms and still be effective for helping workers resolve emotionally intense experiences. It is almost automatic for social workers to exhibit and discuss their feelings. Conversely, due to emotional conditioning—the term used for habits of emotional displays and customs—it is counterculture for police officers to exhibit or admit to displays of tenderness, fear, or sadness.

A case in point occurred in 2009 when the U.S. Army, in reaction to skyrocketing suicide rates among soldiers, implemented training programs designed to teach soldiers how to deal with emotional stress (Carey 2009). The training was designed to head off depression, post-traumatic stress disorder, and suicide, all problems that have plagued twenty percent of the troops returning from Afghanistan and Iraq. Rather than frame the training as emotion management or debriefing or self-care, it was framed as "intensive training in emotional resilience." The army's chief of staff, General George W. Casey Jr., said the program was an effort to transform a military culture that considered talk of emotions to be "so much hand-holding, a sign of weakness" (Carey 2009, p. A1). Like police officials who are grappling with how to help officers cope with emotional stress more effectively in cities across the nation, Pentagon officials wonder whether the army, an organization that has long suppressed talk of emotions, can now reverse that norm.

Out-of-role expressions of emotion define the outer limits of acceptability and draw a zone around the normal. Here a victim advocate describes the worst case she ever worked. It occurred in 1999 when two students brought guns into a high school and shot a number of their classmates. This incident occurred at Columbine High School near Denver, Colorado, and is known among the locals simply as "when Columbine happened."

> I'll just refer back to Columbine. . . . Responding to that was hideous because it was the most chaotic. The trauma was palpable. You could almost see it. You could almost reach out and touch it, and it permeated everybody. There were Denver SWAT officers in tears with that deer-caught-in-the-headlights look, trying to catch a breath. EMS workers—people that ordinarily you don't expect to see fall apart—were falling apart left and right. It was incredibly painful to be there, and the longer the day got, the worse it got because after a while there's a group of parents left here with no kids. There's no bus coming.

The fact that she recalls that SWAT officers were in tears—a situation stunningly outside the norm for the macho nature of SWAT teams—amplifies how extreme this occasion was.

Another issue that arises when a woman works in a traditionally male role or vice versa extends beyond the expectations of coworkers to the expectations of citizens being served. A female flight medic, who had started as a firefighter and who looks younger than her age and is short, five feet two inches, describes the comments she has experienced:

> I mean I look like a kid; I'm short; I'm a girl, so a lot of issues going on. When I first came on I had old-timers tell me stuff. Are you gonna be able to carry the ladder? I said, sir, no. That's why they have four people on the truck. That's why you're here. I'll just be sarcastic like it's so stupid. I mean I'm a firefighter. I am a firefighter. Look it up. I've heard it all.

In addition to teasing and patronizing from teammates, her competence is questioned by a citizen being rescued:

> She was a senior citizen. She was freaked out when she saw me. She goes, "Are you an Explorer?" An Explorer is an extension of Boy Scouts and Girl Scouts. So she thought I was an Explorer riding along on the call. And then she started freaking out when I was doing her IV. And then when I got to drive she asks my partner, "Can she drive this? She's too young to drive." I mean I work here. I just did an IV on you. Come on.

The resistance encountered by this woman was complicated by the fact that she not only was female and physically small but also looked young. On the other hand, the captain of a fire rescue squad says that all members of a squad try to take care of each other. He credits the brotherhood, but then says, "We've got a lot of females in our department—the sisterhood also. That's what we strive for, and it gets everybody looking out for each other, respecting each other, having a good time and everything just kind of takes care of itself."

The work of victim advocates provides the opposite situation. It is patterned after traditional gender relations such that the majority of advocates are female. The process works this way: Workers in a male-dominated field—police officers—are called to a crime scene. Once they see that there is a victim who will benefit from a supportive intervention, the victim advocate is called to the scene. She then sizes up the needs of the victim, creates an environment conducive to talking, and engages the victim in supportive counseling. This happens while police are investigating the crime scene, collecting evidence, and otherwise doing what police do.

Gender differences in emotional expression begin at an early age. From a socialization perspective, boys and girls learn different rules for how and when to express emotion. While boys learn to conceal their feelings, girls learn to more freely express their feelings within socially appropriate boundaries (Brody 1985). These lessons persist through adulthood. The result—emotional conditioning—is demonstrated clearly in the masculine work cultures of law enforcement and firefighting. Both have a male animus that discourages emotional expressivity. Alternately, a female anima suffuses domestic violence work and victim assistance work, giving rise to cultures that encourage emotional expressivity. Thus, masculine work cultures employ critical incident debriefings on an as-needed basis, invoking them only when absolutely necessary. Feminine work cultures employ self-care plans that are continuous and expected to be discussed openly on a continuing basis. In other words, while masculine work cultures isolate emotional expression, feminine cultures integrate it into the everyday workspace.

Gender stereotypes of appropriate behavior are socialized into children's belief systems as early as three to five years of age (Birnbaum 1983). Both mothers and fathers use more varied emotion terms, and more of them, when talking to daughters as compared to talking to sons (Hess et al. 2000). More expressive persons report coming from more expressive family environments. This is noteworthy because conventional wisdom—and the comments of a number of interviewees—suggest that women are more "emotional" than men. In fact, the evidence is that women are more *expressive* than men, but not more emotional. Moreover, differences between boys' and girls' expressiveness emerge after the preschool years and are likely influenced by peers as well as family (Brody 1985). The masking that boys learn, the necessity of concealing their emotions, is not something that most girls learn. In fact, girls are more likely to be reinforced for displaying their feelings.

One gender difference in the performance of emotion work is that women workers who must express an emotion other than what they feel—false-face acting—report more emotional exhaustion and lower job satisfaction than do men who engage in similar levels of pretending. Hazel-Anne Johnson (2007) speculates that the heightened level of inauthenticity is more difficult for women than for men. If it is true that it takes more energy for women to "sit on" one emotion while expressing another, then there are implications for endurance in those jobs where false-face acting is necessary on a regular basis.

The differences between men and women extend beyond a difference in comfort level when suppressing one's own emotion while displaying another. Expressivity refers to the extent to which individuals outwardly display their emotions. Kring and Gordon (1998) conclude that women are more emotionally expressive than men although they do not differ in reports of experienced emotion. Studies suggest that situational circumstances moderate emotional expression, too. This is the function of emotion cultures in the workplace. But, as Hess et al. (2000) remind us, expressivity for women and men is on a continuum; individual personality factors contribute significantly to the degree of expressivity, as do the exigencies of the moment.

When it comes to expressivity, as a general rule, men are internalizers while women are externalizers (Kring & Gordon 1998). This is not a clear-cut distinction, however. In fact, some men are quite expressive and some women are not expressive at all. Additionally, expressivity for both genders varies according to family expressiveness. To a large degree, this means that childhood learning trumps gender in terms of the degree to which emotions are expressed.

Researchers have also found that women and men vary in terms of the specific emotions for which they are more expressive. Particular among these are sadness, disgust, fear, surprise, happiness, and anger. In Kring and Gordon's (1998) experiments, men had greater reactivity to fear and anger while women had greater reactivity to sadness and disgust. In other words, when watching movies that evoked feelings of fear and anger, men showed higher levels of excitation. When watching movies that evoked feelings of sadness and disgust, women showed higher levels of physiological responses. But this expressivity is particularly susceptible to being modified by childhood learning, emotional conditioning, and display rules on the job that make expression explicitly acceptable or unacceptable. An example is a first responder who says it is simply not okay to cry when helping a victim who is crying.

Emotion is expressed not just through words. It also is communicated through facial expression, body language, and touch. Evidence is plentiful that women more accurately identify the meaning of a variety of nonverbal cues, including expression of emotions (Brody & Hall 2008). Touch communicates distinct emotions, and there are gender asymmetries in the process. Hertenstein and Keltner (2010) found that anger is communicated clearly only when a male is either doing the touching or being touched. Sympathy is communicated clearly when a woman is the toucher or the person being touched. Happiness is communicated only if the toucher and the person being touched are both women. The point of these findings is that, for whatever reason, the gender of the communicator matters when touch is used to convey a feeling.

Nonverbal communication has greater impact than verbal. Facial expression alone accounts for 55 percent of the meaning of a message (Mehrabian 2007). When combined with body language, voice inflection, and tone, nonverbal communication accounts for two-thirds of the meaning of a message (Hickson et al. 2004). Both genders employ nonverbal as well as verbal communication, but the nature of the message differs. While women tend to express empathy and openness to feelings, men tend to express tough self-confidence and much less openness to feelings. This fact bleeds over into how male-dominated occupations deal with emotionally intense job experience as compared to how female-dominated occupations deal with it.

In sum, gender differences in emotional expression extend from facial expressions to touch to words. The differences are not black and white, however, and it is not unusual to find a man who is more emotionally expressive than a woman. Early childhood socialization, emotional conditioning, and specific emotion cultures at work combine to produce extremes within both genders. Generally speaking, however, it is safe to say that on average men are less emotionally expressive on the job than are women.

The Wage Penalty

There is a wage penalty for working in emotionally intense jobs. Bhave and Glomb compared salaries for occupations that require emotional labor to occupations that require cognitive labor. Using U.S. Census data, they found statistically significant opposite wage effects. For every one-standard-deviation increase in cognitive demands, there was a wage gain of 6.6 percent, while a one-standard-deviation increase in emotional labor demands was associated with a wage loss of 3.4 percent (2009, p. 698). Then they examined the effects for men versus women wage earners. Their analysis compared salaries of men working in high emotionally demanding jobs to those working in low demand jobs. And then they similarly compared salaries of women. The results for the men revealed a statistically significant negative wage effect for emotional demands, such that a one-standard-deviation increase in demands was accompanied by a decrease of nearly 6 percent in salary. For women, there was also a wage decrement but of a much smaller magnitude, less than 1 percent, which was not statistically significant. This effect was observed after accounting for the proportion of women in each occupation. The researchers found a negative relationship between the proportion of women in a job and wages such that there is a 12 percent wage differential between pay in an all-male occupation and an all-female occupation.

As has long been recognized, wages in male-dominated occupations tend to be higher than in female-dominated occupations (Mastracci 2004). When examining these occupations separately by gender, wages are lower in high emotional labor jobs that are male dominated than in low emotional labor jobs that are male dominated. In contrast, wages in jobs that have high emotional labor demands and are female dominated are no different from wages in jobs with low emotional labor demands that are female dominated. Thus there are different wage effects for men and women based on emotional labor demands. Men are disadvantaged while women are no better nor no worse off than in any other type of job. This is consistent with Guy and Newman's (2004) findings when they investigated salaries of Florida state employees.

The data for men may result from a conflation of two factors: jobs with high emotional labor demands are predominantly in public service. Of the thirty jobs rated highest in emotional labor, almost half are predominantly in the public sector. These include, for example, correctional institution officers, law enforcement officers, dispatchers, social workers, public transportation attendants, administrators in education and related fields, postal clerks, police and detectives, teachers, park guides, therapists, and so forth. Historically, wages in the public and nonprofit sector are lower than in business. It is doubtful that sector alone explains all of the variance, however.

Bhave and Glomb (2009) also studied a number of workers who had changed jobs in order to determine if those who had worked in jobs with high emotional labor demands tended to seek similar work when they changed jobs. Using a longitudinal dataset, the researchers confirmed that this is the case. They found that there is little mobility between occupations from high to low emotional labor demands and vice versa. This was true for both women and men. Rather, occupational switches for both genders are often to jobs with similar levels of emotive demands. These findings are consistent with those of Hsieh (2009). He studied midlevel public managers and found that their self-report of compassion was a better predictor of their emotive effort on the job than agency display rules were. This would indicate that workers, regardless of gender, who score high in compassion will seek jobs that allow them to express it. Jobs high in emotional labor demands provide just such an outlet.

Questions That Beg to Be Answered

There are a multitude of questions that remain to be answered about the performance of emotionally intense work. Among them are these: What is the interaction of formal power and emotional expressivity when the responder is in uniform? What is the effect of demographic difference when the worker is engaging with the citizen in emotion work? What is the effect of nontraditional gender behavior as compared to traditional gender role behavior? We turn to discussion of each.

The Effect of Uniforms

It is accepted fact that uniforms and stripes make it easy to identify who the squad leader is. But do they also affect the nature of emotional expression both for those who wear them and for citizens being assisted by them? Although this topic has not been researched, there are hints. For example, the account below was given by a female victim advocate and describes how she collaborates with a police officer, usually a man, in uniform when it is necessary to make a home visit to notify someone of a death:

> The protocol is that if an outside agency calls the police and says we want you to notify someone in your city of a death, we've trained the police officers to get that information directly from the reporting agency rather than through dispatch so they have good, accurate information, call an advocate at the same time, we meet with the police officer ahead of time down the road a little bit, strategize about how we're going to do the death notification and what information is had and who the next of kin is. Go to the door, knock on it, police officer introduces himself, could we come in? We have some important information for you. Textbook case, we get to come into the living room, advocate looks around and if there's kids or anything like that we may say would you mind if we took your kids into the other room while the officer talks to you about some important information to just not have the kids there or if they're not there we would sit with them, officer tells the loved one that their person has died. We train them to use the word "dead," not "passed away" or "we've lost them" or anything like that because euphemisms can sometimes serve to keep denial in place and so we train around that and then we're there to address the emotional needs and the practical needs after that. The officer is there not only to lend credibility to the news but to ensure safety to the victim who we're notifying and of the advocate because you never know how people are going to react and there could—they could fall down with a heart attack or they could start beating you up, or they could run down the road or they could just fall on the floor and cry or they could just be still. However they do it, it's just everybody deals with that in a different way, but we want to be prepared for whatever happens.

In this situation we see several examples of how cultural norms shape the performance of emotional labor. First, a man and a woman go together to the call. The man wears a uniform and is the authority figure. The woman, especially if she takes children into another room, plays the role of mother/ nurturer. Together they simulate and reproduce traditional gender roles and use the uniform to transmit a message of authority.

Diverse versus Homogeneous Dyads

We do not know the effect of demographic homogeneous dyads as compared to heterogeneous dyads (Hispanic-Anglo; male-male; female-female; female-male; black-white) on the controlled expression of emotion. We do not know the impact on the citizen when a responder displays emotion that is counter to traditional gender roles. Beyond a focus on gender, we do not know about other forms of diversity, such as race, ethnicity, or age, and how they affect the communication of emotion from the service provider to the citizen. For instance, is it correct to assume citizens will respond best to a provider who is of the same background or same skin color? Is it correct to assume that providers prefer to be of the same background or same skin color? We do not know if rapport is more easily established in one type of dyad as compared to another. If we did know that, it would be helpful when staffing emergency medical services and assigning crews to geographic zones according to demographics.

Gender Roles

Although we tend to lump all public service agencies together and then talk about gender, we are mistaken to do so. What we do not know is what effect occurs in terms of emotional coping when a woman is in charge of a traditionally male work unit, such as a team of firefighters. Are critical incident debriefings used more frequently? Do outcomes of interventions differ based on whether responders' roles are aligned with traditional gender roles or not? In other words, what differences in outcomes, if any, result when the workforce extends beyond tradition? All these questions and more are important if we are to understand the dynamics that lie beneath the surface in terms of service provision and outcomes during emotionally intense situations.

Summary

The legitimacy of state action comes to the foreground in the work of first responders. Citizens must trust strangers to enter their homes and do their work. Authority and competence are important attributes that suffuse the work of responders. Visual cues, such as uniforms, help to imbue responders with the power of the state. At the same time, the fact that they represent the state adds a responsibility on the part of responders to measure up to citizens' expectations.

Emotional labor is performed in a manner that is consistent with cultural expectations. Norms sculpt the way that women and men express emotions, and work cultures amplify these norms. A masculine culture, such as police work, embraces one notion of appropriate and inappropriate emotional expression, while a feminine culture, such as social work, embraces another. Gender roles define men as authority figures and women as nurturers. For example, job segregation causes men to work predominantly in roles where they are to be tough and authoritative. Women predominantly work in roles where they are to be nurturant and empathic. Although there is no difference in the amount of emotional labor that men and women perform, there is a difference in how they operate and which emotions they express.

Gender makes a difference not only in the performance of emotional labor, but also in how workers cope with the emotional intensity of their jobs. While women who work in jobs predominated by women are more likely to discuss emotions easily and to use self-care plans, those who work in jobs predominated by men are more likely to be constrained in their facility with emotions. Understanding these differences is the first step in knowing what sort of interventions will be most helpful in creating a means by which first responders can deal constructively with vicarious trauma and post-traumatic stress disorder.

Private sector jobs that require emotional labor are more pacific than public service jobs. In the private sector, such jobs use emotional labor to read a customer's mood and adjust communication so as to effect a sale or elicit a hospitable reaction in a usual business transaction. Public service jobs use emotional labor more often under conditions of great emotional intensity, such as in crises. And the legitimacy of government action comes into play. There must be trust and the judicious use of power. As with most public services, demographic differences between those who deliver the service and those who are being served are important. The element of job segregation results in distinct emotion cultures. For men, there is a wage penalty in jobs that are emotionally intense. Men's salaries are lower when they work in high emotional demand jobs than if they work in standard men's jobs. This wage penalty does not obtain for women, however. Their wages remain at the same depressed rate whether they work in high emotional demand jobs or not.

In sum, the characteristics of the people who perform emotional labor, and how they perform it, are directly relevant to the power, authority, and legitimacy of the state. The traditional subjects of representative bureaucracy directly enter into the discussion because of the personal dynamics involved in the rapport between responder and citizen. Trust and confidence in governmental actors are essential if citizens are to rely on responders and defer to their authority during the response.

7

Professional Standards and Discretion in Crisis Response

One early winter evening on Chicago's northwest side, officer Martin Preib and his partner responded to a call. At the scene, they encountered a young man wearing gang colors followed by his girlfriend, who alleged that he hit her and she wanted to have him arrested. Officer Prieb thought to himself, "Battery victims are rarely so demanding, so defiant. She sounds rehearsed, prepared" (2010, p. 57). He and his partner separated the two and started asking questions, still not knowing who the victim was or whether a crime occurred at all. After gathering information, the officer made a judgment call (Preib 2010, p. 58, emphasis original):

> A few years ago her plan might have worked. I would have concluded we had no choice but to arrest him, for she had sufficiently created all the elements of a crime: an allegation, an alleged victim, an offender, signed complaints. Even if we thought they were false, I would have blindly followed the law. *Not tonight, sweetheart. No way.*

In this incident, Officer Preib and his partner sized up the situation, decided that the accuser was not telling the truth, and chose not to press charges against her boyfriend.

In contrast to this scenario, "mandatory-arrest" policies require responding officers to apprehend an accused offender outright rather than to force the accuser to decide whether or not to press charges. Twenty-one states have enacted mandatory-arrest laws and another nine states have "pro-arrest" policies, which encourage officers to default toward arrest when in doubt (ABA 2007).[1] Mandatory- and pro-arrest policies are "intended to provide immediate protection for the victim, deter the abuser from future acts of violence, and relieve the victim of the responsibility of making a difficult decision under possibly difficult circumstances to press charges" (Phillips & Sobel 2010).

They are examples of bureaucratic reforms intended to exorcise discretion via direct codification of decision making. Maynard-Moody and Musheno (2003, p. 14) observe that "police abuse in New York City has led to new guidelines for interacting with the public, even including pocket-sized script cards to prompt good manners." The guidelines have the added effect of restricting the degree of emotional labor needed to engage with the public (Wharton 2009).

Cameras and microphones record everything Chicago police officers say and do throughout the duration of their twelve-hour shifts (Preib 2010). Heightened bureaucratic controls are meant to eliminate discretion and improve outcomes. In the case of mandatory- and pro-arrest laws, the goal is to reduce domestic violence. Unintended consequences of these laws have included dual arrest, a situation in which the victim not only suffers from abuse but also now has legal troubles, and retaliatory arrest, where no abuse occurs but abuse allegations are made in order to get back at someone else, leading to a false arrest (Frye, Haviland, & Rajah 2007). Officer Preib and his partner concluded that the above situation was just such a case: The alleged victim was mad at her boyfriend and intended to put the police in the middle of their fight, to use the law as a weapon and, in the officer's estimation, clog the courts, fill the jails, and lengthen arrest records. He tells the girlfriend (Preib 2010, pp. 59–60):

> Look at me. Listen carefully. You're going to get yourself in trouble. You think you can use this to get back at him, but this isn't the first domestic dispute we've been to. We know when they are legitimate and when they are not.

But who are *they* to decide whether abuse took place or not? How do they know? Do we want officers to make judgment calls like this? What if Illinois were, in fact, a mandatory-arrest state—would these officers have broken the law by talking the girlfriend out of making an abuse allegation, which happens even in jurisdictions with mandatory-arrest laws (Phillips & Sobel 2010)? Or rather, should officers "blindly follow the law," as Officer Preib wondered? The classic depiction of impartial Justice is a woman, blindfolded, holding a scale. Exercising discretion is to peek through that blindfold. Is this justice denied?

In this chapter, we review the debate on administrative discretion in public administration. Related issues were discussed in Chapter 5 as well. What should guide its exercise, given the need for discretion in the implementation and enforcement of public law? One view is that the rule of law alone should guide the exercise of discretion, for anything else undermines representative democracy. Another view is that the law can be wrong sometimes, and professional codes of conduct ought to guide discretionary decision making. We find that, among crisis responders, professional codes of conduct hold substantial sway over decision making in general and therefore also over the exercise of discretion. We demonstrate why this is the case in crisis response and conclude that the exercise of discretion requires emotional labor, and because administrative rules are largely blind to emotional labor—as shown in Chapter 2—professional norms must guide discretion. We conclude this chapter with a discussion of the downside of discretion that emanates from strong identification with one's teammates.

The Debate on Discretion

Whether administrative discretion is justice denied or served depends upon whom you ask. Although concerns about administrative discretion predate the founding of the nation (Haque 2004), most observers situate the debate in terms set by Carl Friedrich (1940) and Herman Finer (1941). Friedrich argues that administrative discretion is not only inevitable, but necessary and beneficial, and he goes so far as to place it at the very center of policy making: "Public policy is being formed as it is being executed, and it is likewise being executed as it is being formed" (1940, p. 6). Street-level workers "actualize policy" (Maynard-Moody & Musheno 2003, p. 11). Care should be taken in the exercise of discretion because "exceptions have a way of becoming accepted practices, as every bureaucrat knows" (Stivers 2008, p. 4). The exercise of discretion—of making exceptions—can manifest as spoils and patronage (Battaglio & Condrey 2009), favoritism toward certain race, ethnic, or gender groups (Sowa & Selden 2003; Scott 1997), shirking or sabotage (Brehm & Gates 1997), or innovation and leadership (Vinzant & Crothers 1998). Discretion can be used well or poorly, but it cannot be eliminated altogether (Friedrich 1940). Brodkin argues that the exercise of discretion is in fact necessary to good governance (2007, p. 2):

> For all practical purposes, policy implementation rests in the hands of the social workers, teachers, police, nurses, counselors, and caseworkers ostensibly at the bottom of the policy hierarchy. . . . Typical street-level bureaucrats maintain a certain amount of irreducible discretion, in part, because their individual interactions with clients largely occur outside of direct observation. . . . The bureaucracy problem is not that discretion exists, but that neither policymakers, administrators, nor agency clients can trust that it will be used well.

Thus, Brodkin's view is consistent with that of Friedrich, who argues that administrative discretion "had arisen in response to undeniable needs, and that therefore the real problem is how to render [administrators] responsible, not how to take all power away from them" (1940, p. 10). Friedrich further observes that administrators exercise discretion in accordance with their professional judgment and "attach so little weight to the influence of parliamentary or legislative bodies" (1940, p. 8). Friedrich concludes that the professional standards of administrators hold far greater sway over their decisions than do the standard operating procedures and rules of the agency or department for which they work, and that this is sufficient to secure responsible conduct of public administrators.

Finer, on the other hand, fails to see how professional standards of conduct could possibly ensure democratic responsibility. He argues that the "desire to be approved by his fellow officials" is no replacement for accountability to the public through its democratically elected representatives. In response to Friedrich's assertion that professional norms are enough to curb bad behavior, Finer argues (1941, p. 336, emphasis supplied):

> Servants of the public *are not* to decide their own course; they are to be responsible to the elected representatives of the public, and these are to determine the course of action of the public servants *to the most minute degree* that is technically feasible.

To Finer, running afoul of the rule of law is far more deleterious to democracy than is failing to earn the esteem of one's peers: "The one implies public execution, the other hara-kiri" (1941, p. 336). Friedrich argues that either the threat of public execution or the prospect of hara-kiri—or both—are sufficient to control the use of discretion; in fact, where one leaves off, the other picks up. Others build upon this argument to add the concept of prudence as it guides the exercise of discretion (Dobel 1990; Kane & Patapan 2006). Where laws and standard operating procedures fail to regulate action in a situation, professional norms substitute. For Friedrich (1940, p. 22), this is appropriate and preferable, because rules cannot cover every contingency and sometimes "the rule is at fault," which is precisely the principle underpinning administrative evil, as defined by Adams, Balfour, and Reed (2006). "A few bad apples" would define the abuse of discretion, but in their study of Abu Ghraib prison, they found that it was not the exercise of discretion that was the problem. In this case it was following orders (p. 682):

> Indeed, ordinary people may simply be acting appropriately in their organizational role—in essence, just doing what those around them would agree they should be doing—and at the same time, participating in what a critical and reasonable observer, usually well after the fact, would call evil.

Similarly, Stivers (2008, p. 45) explains how following rules—not exercising discretion—undermined democratic ideals in Vichy France during World War II: "Lawyers chose to exert themselves finding loopholes and ambiguities in anti-Semitic laws rather than protesting their existence." And more recently, in reference to the administration of President George W. Bush (p. 37):

> Bush administration lawyers had been laboring to construct arguments justifying extreme latitude in the treatment of those captured in the "global war on terror." These arguments focused on techniques of interrogation, conditions of imprisonment, and methods by which the legal system would process prisoners or keep them incarcerated indefinitely.

Lest the typical public servant—including those committed to saving lives like our crisis responders—reject the notion that "the question of torture [is] directly relevant to their duties or the meaning of their lives in public service," Stivers further asserts (p. 37, emphasis supplied):

> Torture reveals the link between power and truth in governance. The spectacle of abused bodies in state-sponsored prisons confronts *every person who exercises state power* with the need to reflect on just how far that power can go . . . just how far each of us is prepared to go.

Her point is that following the rules is not enough to guarantee right action or democratic representation because, in the first instance, the rules can be wrong and can mask administrative evil, and in the second instance, the people's representatives might not be clear about how a policy is to be implemented. This second point undermines Finer's argument that, if a policy comes from democratically elected representatives, it must necessarily reflect the will of the people, but that might not be enough if the law is not specific enough with respect to implementation. In his analysis of the national health service corps, Frank Thompson concludes that no one set out to flout the law, but rather that the law lacked clarity on day-to-day operations (1982, p. 440):

> There is no evidence to suggest that the corps flagrantly broke the law or was grossly unaccountable. Statutory goals were vague, and the intent behind the legislation was subject to multiple interpretations. The corps capitalized on the discretion permitted by the statute, but it did not go beyond the law.

This is also observed by Evelyn Brodkin, remarking on welfare policy. Interestingly, Brodkin seems to suggest that the ostensibly sacrosanct will of the people—à la Finer—may be obfuscated intentionally by the people's representatives themselves, perhaps for political reasons (2007, p. 3):

Legislators have a tendency to delegate down the more contentious specifics of social policy. In effect, that shifts policymaking from an overt politics of the legislative process to an indirect politics of administrative practice.

So what are public servants to do? If they are not to rely on the rules, then what? Friedrich argues that professional standards, the administrator's version of peer review, should be the arbiter of discretionary action: "before the goddess of science all men are equal" (1940, p. 23). "But when Professor Friedrich advocates the official's responsibility to 'the fellowship of science,'" counters Finer, "the result to be feared is the enhancement of official conceit and what has come to be known as 'the new despotism'" (Finer 1941, p. 340). An extreme example of the perversion of professional standards such that it produces administrative evil is found in Robert Jay Lifton's meticulous and harrowing account of "the medicalization of killing—the imagery of killing in the name of healing" (1986, p. 14) that was endorsed and carried out by Nazi doctors to protect the *Volk*, the body of the whole German people. Lifton quotes one Nazi doctor as saying (p. 16), "Of course I am a doctor and I want to preserve life. And out of a respect for human life, I would remove a gangrenous appendix from a diseased body. The Jew is the gangrenous appendix in the body of mankind."

Obviously, this is an extreme example, but Finer in fact drew from his observations of Hitler's Germany to argue against the exercise of administrative discretion using professional norms. The point is, however, that the role of professional standards in the service of the state warrants added scrutiny of any action of the state. The implications of discretion are amplified for the same reasons that we gave earlier for the importance of emotional labor in public service vis-à-vis the private sector: Government is the only game in town for vulnerable populations and for certain goods and services. Finer passionately underscores the responsibility not only of holding monopoly power, but also of funding that power with other people's money (1941, p. 342):

My own studies . . . of local and central government officials in Great Britain have taught me what a great power for the good can be exercised by them. . . . But even with this we must require principally and austerely the subservience of the public official. Without this requirement, we shall gradually slip into a new version of taxation without representation. . . . We shall become subject to what has, in a short time, almost always been to the detriment of the public welfare—producer's control of the products, the services, the commodities which the producer thinks are good for the consumer and ought to be produced at the consumer's expense.

What Finer describes here, of course, is the concept of the public good or service, which we discussed at length in Chapter 1. The responsibility of exercising discretion while holding monopoly power and spending other people's money is understood by some, as this police officer in Miami articulates:

> I was taught as a child to whom much is given, much is required . . . and so I have to police myself. I have to remind myself constantly that I have to live up to the expectations that there are. . . . I haven't done anything criminal but there are times when I have to challenge myself: "Are you living up to those expectations?" And yes, there are times that I fall short.

In the paragraphs that follow, we will examine a number of questions related to the discretion that emergency responders exercise when performing their job. How do they act at the moment of crisis? How do they decide how to act? We will investigate the individual, personalized strategies of employing emotional labor in instantaneous decision making and judgment calls. Based on our interviews, we conclude that crisis responders exhibit behavior predicted by Carl Friedrich. They rely on professional norms more than on agency rules. This is due in large part to the powerful influence of their professional socialization via promotions through occupational ranks, a paramilitary chain of command, long-standing traditions, teammate influence, and identifying with the profession (Guy 1985). The crisis responder acts in accordance with, in Friedrich's words, "a sense of duty [and] a desire to be approved by his fellow officials" (1940, p. 8).

Since this book is devoted to the "how" question as it relates to emotional labor, the question in this chapter is "How do crisis responders exercise discretion in contexts that demand substantial exertion of emotional labor?" Our conclusion points to professional standards because, to a person, crisis responders identified principally with their profession and their team rather than their jurisdiction. We then provide examples of what this looks like in action. We conclude with a discussion of the implications of relying on professional norms to determine discretionary actions in public service.

Crisis Response as Identity, Vocation, and Family Tradition

According to Maynard-Moody and Musheno (2003, p. 51),

> Street-level workers have strong occupational identities that help them maneuver through the workday. Having only light supervision, they rely on standard operating procedures and commonly understood norms to guide their decisions. Particularly for occupations of long standing, such as social

work, police work, and firefighting, conventional wisdom holds that the bonds of occupational identity are highly salient, creating a local culture of shared beliefs that enable them to handle tensions in the workplace and risks on the job.

While this observation embraces all occupations in crisis response, it is particularly applicable to sworn officers and those who work in uniform. Sworn officers are never really "off duty" and uniformed officials visually communicate the power of the state. This is further imprinted by the paramilitary occupations of police and firefighters with their hierarchical, command-and-control structure of rank and promotions. Symbols like uniforms and regalia denote rank and amplify the sense that "we're all in this together" and "it's us against the world." Aside from the uniforms, ranks, and the nature of the work, jobs in emergency services are fundamentally different from other types of jobs because of their intensity. Those who hold these jobs are extraordinarily committed. We observed this across contexts and across occupational categories, throughout emergency services. One man in Chicago speaks about an event that affected a fellow officer:

> He just was going to Notre Dame to pick up his daughter a couple weeks ago, and while going there he came upon an accident and he had to actually hold a patient, he got blood all over him and everything but, you know, what are you going to do? You've got to do what you're trained to do and so you're—are you ever off duty?

No. One is never off duty. Another responder told us,

> As a representative of the state, I have a legal and ethical responsibility to respond and to take care of people, and I believe that most of the people in here have a strong moral character and moral fiber, so we can't pass a car scene and *not* help because we have the skills to help.

But the sense of obligation and identification with one's calling goes deeper, as articulated beautifully by a firefighter for Miami-Dade Fire Rescue:

> There is a symbolic brotherhood amongst the emergency responders. Perhaps it's through understanding of each other's highs and lows and the nature of the job that we tend to gravitate more to each other during down times by being able to discuss things, being able to listen and being able to visualize similar actions that have occurred . . . there is a significant brotherhood that has existed for many, many, many years in the fire service, and I feel a part of that brotherhood.

And despite the undeniable level of dedication that is required to devote one's career—one's life—to crisis response, we heard time and again that this is not a choice made begrudgingly. Not at all. The sacrifice is chosen, the duty embraced. A police officer recalls how she feels when she has been on the scene when a person dies:

> I feel better about myself and my life when I'm helping someone else, and [being with someone at the time of their death] is an opportunity to help people . . . and some of them are so horribly alone that it's just sad, and to be present with somebody at that moment, that's a gift.

These men and women *are* emergency responders; they do not *work as* emergency responders or *in* emergency response. To a person, our respondents identified themselves as their occupations. What's more, many felt they were born into it: "I'm a third-generation firefighter in this department—we've got probably three or four more others probably third- or fourth-generation firefighters [in this unit] . . . it's something they came up through the family." Crisis response is not a job—it's a calling and, sometimes, a family tradition. When asked to describe their jobs and when asked to whom they feel responsible and accountable, our respondents invariably spoke of service to people and dedication to their fellow crisis responders, be they firefighters, police officers, or EMTs. The men and women we interviewed who had been promoted to administrative work felt as though they were no longer doing what they were trained to do—help people—but most found satisfaction knowing that they can supervise and train newer generations of crisis responders.

> Why do you want to be a firefighter? . . . Everyone says, "I want to help people." You're the doctor, you're the policeman, you're the public servant. If you don't have that in your heart that you want to help someone, you're not there. It's not [about] *you*. It's for them. That goes back ages. You're there to help, and I think everybody has that in their heart. That's why they start. It's not for the shift; it's not for the money.

Pulling Rank: The Command-and-Control Structure of Crisis Response

The strict hierarchy in crisis response makes sense given the chaotic, dangerous nature of the work. There simply cannot be several people in control simultaneously. Emergency services developed as paramilitary agencies with top-down, command-and-control structures. These traditions affect the way that discretion is exercised by responders. On the scene, the chain of command is absolute: "Everybody knows that . . . in this type of organization there is a chain of command. You must follow it." Only safety concerns can trump the chain of command, and even that is a fairly recent development in the fire services, as noted by this firefighter:

> When you're on an emergency call, it's a dictatorship. That's it. . . . Let's say you're a firefighter on a call and you're doing an operation and you see something that's life threatening, you have the right to stop it right now. Every person has the right to stop something that they feel is dangerous, and that's a good thing because if the chief's up front, [he] can't see everything going on and you see something going on—boom—stop it right now. Everybody has the right to do that. You didn't have that in the old days. Now you have that right and if you feel it's dangerous, nobody's going to question it. Pull out. It's a safety thing.

This point was echoed by a firefighter in Miami:

> In times of an emergency we embark on almost an authoritarian-style form of leadership where there isn't much discussion back and forth unless there is something outright that's perceived as a safety issue—something that is terribly wrong that the officer wasn't able to recognize.

The command-and-control structure of emergency services is sustained through the use of standardized rankings within the organizational hierarchy—rankings that are labeled using military titles like "battalion chief," "lieutenant," and "sergeant." One officer recalls,

> We are taught that restraint in our hierarchy is part of our job unless it's an outstanding safety grievance . . . we are taught that we have to maintain that restraint through stepping back and minding our tongue.

He was taught this through examples demonstrated by other officers who respected the rankings of their superiors. The hierarchical structure ultimately performs a safety function as well (emphasis supplied):

> There definitely has to be clearly someone in charge that everybody respects; otherwise a lot of freelancing occurs and then it just can turn to chaos very quickly. . . . If you don't already have [control] before you get on scene, it can be difficult and a lot of times it's just a matter of everybody being professional and doing their job and *respecting the rank structure*.

Rankings are manifested in uniforms and regalia, which indicate who is in command to the public and to other crisis responders. The worker's physical appearance is regulated in the uniformed services, from uniforms to rules about visible tattoos, piercings, hair color, and facial hair. Appearance is taken seriously: "If you come in here and your dress clothes are wrinkled and your shoes aren't shined and your hair—you're not feeling any respect for that job." This is part of embodying the role, not just doing a job. Rafaeli and Sutton (1988) and Rafaeli (1989) find that workers who wear uniforms adhere to professional norms of conduct to a greater degree than do workers not in uniform, regardless of gender or job. A firefighter with Miami-Dade Fire Rescue explains how uniforms help to uphold the command-and-control structure on the scene:

> There's a lot of imagery in the service. It not only identifies, sets us apart from, victims maybe on an accident, it gives, you know, almost like a—kind of a beacon [that says], "These are the people that are here to help me." I can clearly identify them and then that uniform plays its role and identification within the workers themselves. We have different color helmets. We have different vehicles, things like that, so we kinda stratify amongst ourselves as well as the public. We separate ourselves. [The] uniform—it clearly does have a role.

The uniform communicates assistance—salvation even. It is a "beacon" but it also conveys authority to workers in order to organize the crisis scene, as the firefighter describes above, and it sorts out "who's who." But the primary authority message sent by the uniform is from the state to the citizenry. The uniform is authority and therefore the individual wearing the uniform embodies authority. So much so, according to this Illinois State Police sergeant, that his own identity melds with the uniform:

> I never get challenged with the hat—even the CPD [Chicago Police Department] guys tell us that we have the coolest hats. If you tilt it up enough in the back you can't see your eyes or if you wear sunglasses, people don't even look at your face, so you come up the side of the car like [Joe Don Baker in] *Walking Tall* and their eyes go right up to the hat. The "Smokey the Bear" hat almost *takes your face away.*

Similarly, Hsieh and Hsieh (2010), studying police officers in a jurisdiction that had not previously required them to include surnames on their uniforms, found that the officers strongly preferred relative anonymity, which preserved their sense of security in their exercise of authority. Roles are conveyed outward to the public but also within the hierarchy. As in the military, rankings are meaningful in that insubordination can lead to penalties or dismissal, as one supervisor's story about an emergency incident illustrates:

> When the call was over, first thing when we were finished, in my office and he sat down and I sat down. We had a little talk. [I told him] Don't ever publicly disobey or question my order. That's insubordination. I said, in the military I would have fired you on the scene and get you replaced.

It is not uncommon for crisis responders to have military experience, and the command-and-control structure is effective for leading in crisis situations. By way of example, in the fire services, the number of bugles or stars on shirt collar pins denotes rank. A high-ranking officer recounts a situation when he had to reinforce the hierarchy in order to administer effectively:

> We have staff meetings and sometimes a person will just go on and on and on about something and, you know what? That's enough. . . . Count these. I've got five. You got none. Shut up.[2]

Authority is reciprocal and is reinforced by the uniform, as another fire chief observed when he was promoted into a position where the previous chief chose not to wear the uniform. This was a sore spot with the rank and file:

> Ninety-five percent of the time I wear my uniform. . . . To me [it means that] I'm being recognized as the Chief and [it] must mean something to them because they recognize that and they've commented on it a number of times . . . they know who their leader is, I guess . . . and [that] you're with them. You're dressed like them; you are part of the team.

Haise and Rucker (2003) also found workers to prefer wearing formal uniforms because they felt it afforded them greater authority. In crisis response, pulling rank—reinforcing the hierarchy—is done principally for safety reasons and sometimes in the interests of administrative expedience, but not often for the sake of merely reinforcing the hierarchy. Pulling rank for the sake of doing so can backfire with civilian employees, as an officer with Miami-Dade Fire Rescue notes. He contrasts his personal management style with the

> Very vertical type of leadership which is the military. I understand that probably because they have to sometimes deal with emergencies. That happens. But as I said, by nature that's not my management style at all, but you do have to be flexible.

This opens the door for the exercise of discretion. Given the simultaneously unstructured/structured nature of emergency response, the way discretion is exercised and the types of issues or matters over which discretion is exercised will be unique. Furthermore, the nature of emergency response as a calling, coupled with the standardization of skill sets in emergency services across jurisdictions, results in discretion being informed by professional norms as well as standard operating procedures.

Exercising Discretion in Crisis Response

Emergency responders look to each other when it comes to on-the-job decision making. Strong professional identity was also found in the forest service studied by Kaufman (1960) and revisited by Koontz (2007). This identity, bolstered by strict reliance on the agency's procedure manual, facilitated the use of discretion, as did the relative homogeneity of the forest rangers. Similar backgrounds led to similar worldviews, which, coupled with strong occupational norms, led to similar ideas about the job and priorities. Our crisis responders cite experience repeatedly as the principal source of guidance for their jobs—their own work experience and that of their colleagues. This officer's comments characterize what we heard from many crisis responders when asked how they exercise discretion:

> A lot of it comes from experience . . . through the stories of other people and what's gone good and what's gone bad from them you learn from that, and you have to take every opportunity you can get whether it's actually your experiences on scene and going back and talking with your crews afterwards [and asking], "Hey, how could we do this differently, did we get lucky here, did we do the right thing, did things go well?"—and trying to elicit that from other people and hear their stories is a huge part of it. . . . It's something you just get better with as you do it.

> *Interviewer: To what extent is discretion part of . . . formal training?*

> Very little. I think the officer development program right now . . . it's either eighty or one hundred and twenty hours [on] a lot of things about policies and procedures. . . . [Exercising discretion] is something that's very difficult to teach because every scene is different and every incident is going to be different. You can pull up to the same fire twice and it could go totally different both times.

So workers rely on each other, which is not surprising given the substantial legitimacy and credibility granted by responders to the socialization and promotion processes in their occupations. They are their own most credible sources for information on workplace decision making. Despite administrative rules and regulations meant to control the use of discretion, such as the mandatory- and pro-arrest policies defined at the beginning of this chapter, the need for judgment calls will always exist. A supervisor in Chicago observes the tension between the need to follow orders and the need to give his EMTs autonomy:

> We've got an eighty-eight-page document of standard operating procedures but not everything fits neatly into those different procedures so you may have a patient that has multiple issues that aren't going to fit neatly into a procedure so I think you have to give them the discretion and ability to make those decisions on their own . . . but understand, and they understand too, that they're working within a framework or guidelines of protocols and that there are certain things that they can't deviate from, but there is possibility that they end up making [judgment] calls too.

Another Chicago responder provides a specific example of exercising discretion on the scene and basing his decision making on experience rather than rules:

> With our experience and our expertise we know how much the situation is changing by the change in the smoke, smoke conditions, color of the smoke, just the conditions that you see from when you get there . . . that's the time that you've got to make a decision. You've got to manage the risk . . . instead of going offensive, you're going to take the guys out because it's too risky and you're going to go defensive. . . . Could be [a matter of] seconds . . . or minutes, it depends.

His colleague provides an example when split-second decision making is literally a matter of life and death, when safety trumps standard operating procedures:

> You might pull up on an incident where . . . you've got heavy black smoke showing . . . there are cars in the driveway so you may think there's some-body in the building, but from a risk analysis standpoint you almost have to say, "You know what? The people in there are probably dead" and you've got to make the decision because you can't risk the safety of your own people going in under those conditions. It might not be worth the risk and that's why you've got to manage that in your subconscious. It's a tough decision to make.

Given the deep level of commitment and dedication possessed by crisis responders, the exercise of discretion becomes easier to appreciate. Crisis responders exercise discretion in life-or-death situations, as the two examples above illustrate, but they also make decisions that affect lives in subtler ways. In the discussion of accountability in Chapter 5, we heard from an officer in Miami who equated the power he possesses with that of the president of the United States. In fact, he said that from the point of view of someone he has apprehended, he actually has more power than the president. Here is another example in which the law enforcement officer consults with a colleague; in other words, he relies on the guidance of a superior officer rather than the letter of the law to guide his decision:

> There are a lot of cases where you knew kids have done something and that putting them in jail would create a situation where they would go to jail time and time again and more people would get hurt in the long run . . . and so my thought was if I could figure out a way to [punish them without sending them to jail] and I had a supervisor that helped me with that discretion—guided my course—we decided [to] find a way to limit their involvement with the criminal justice system and sort of create a diversionary program of our own.

In the following example, a Chicago police officer and his partner weigh the pros and cons of following the letter of the law by arresting a suspect against the cost to them, which in this case amounts to two or three hours off their beat (Preib 2010, p. 106):

> We debate taking him in. Having no ID, we will likely have to process him, fill out the many computer screens of information, then wait for approval from the desk sergeant, then the watch commander. He is also wearing a boatload of jewelry, which, under new order, must be inventoried separately from other possessions. Two hours? Three? Is the lockup busy and backed up? Besides, they cooperated. No, we'll cut him, the decision I make more and more these days.

Officer Preib and his partner weigh the benefits of arresting the guy and getting him off the street against the costs to them of several hours away from their beat, resulting in their decision to cut him loose. Similarly, another responder gives an example of how following the letter of the law might be right in the short run, but produce less-than-optimal outcomes in the long run. Moreover, as a supervisor, he allows his subordinates the same level of latitude that he prefers for himself:

> Rules are *guidelines*, okay? They are not hard and fast. . . . The rule says patient goes to the hospital. No. What if the patient doesn't need to go to

the hospital, okay? But you can take that patient to the hospital and be clear in fifteen minutes but it's going to take me an hour and a half to sit and talk to their social worker and their physician but that's the "right" thing to do. In other words, I always tell people—guys in the field—if you can justify your actions by doing something for the patient, for the crew, for the department, or for the county, you will get my support. If you're telling me . . . "We took this patient to Broward County because that's where they wanted to go," you don't have to say anymore. That's good. You're covered and I'm all for that. Rules are guidelines.

This supervisor put the objective, the goal, of any incident before the rules—if one of his people breaks the rules for the patient, the crew, the department, or the county, then he's "all for that." He accords his people the level of discretion that he exercises, which demonstrates his personal theory of justice in the exercise of street-level discretion (Kelly 1994).

This example demonstrates a high level of communication and structure in the exercise of discretion. Extensive training using incident simulations helps workers to anticipate situations and exercise discretion in order to minimize negative outcomes and maximize positive outcomes. But some situations are difficult to simulate or rare enough that simulating them seems impractical, given the scarcity of training time and resources. The following is a dramatic example of a crisis responder in a unique situation who, rather than making a judgment call, decides to "blindly follow the law." In this incident, a U.S. Coast Guard officer in Miami describes what happened when a junior officer encountered people trying to enter the country illegally:

> You see the lengths people go to try and make it [to the United States]. . . the ones who come up with all kinds of innovative ways to build a boat and try and make it . . . they get close and you've got to stop them, and those are hard . . . but you can't let them land. . . . The "Surfside Six" were six people in a raft and they got close enough that the Monday morning news helicopters were out there, the Coast Guard boat's out there, and these guys are right off the beach, and they're close enough that they can actually swim in and put a foot on dry land and . . . [here comes a] probably twenty-year-old Coast Guard [officer]—he's been trained, but he never really got trained in that situation. He comes [and] pepper sprays the people in the water. . . . You try and stop them well offshore and not let the situation escalate to where . . . people are fighting for their lives.

It is assumed that a government agency would get into trouble when its people exercise discretion, not when they follow the rules. The crisis responder above failed to mention that the young officer was not the only official attempting to repel the refugees—news footage captured images of Coast Guard boats using fire hoses to push back their raft as well. The incident did not involve just one young, misguided officer unilaterally enforcing the rules. Both incidents prompted discussion of the U.S. government's "wet foot/dry foot" policy, whereby Cubans intercepted at sea are returned to Cuba, while those who reach U.S. land are paroled into the United States and can apply for permanent residency after one year. In this case, "Don't let them land," as an absolute injunction, was deemed wrong.

Emotional Labor, Professional Norms, and the Exercise of Discretion

The exercise of discretion requires emotional labor: reading the situation, sizing up how the people involved are feeling, anticipating outcomes, and measuring one's own affect and reactions. Because administrative rules are blind to emotional labor, as discussed in Chapter 2, responders consult their coworkers. Norms are accorded substantial legitimacy and are reinforced through symbols like ranks and titles. And the longer that team members work together, the more they see things similarly and agree on decisions (Guy 1985). The downside for responders is this: Camaraderie through intimate identification with one's occupation and teammates can evolve into isolation. The "thin blue line" representing law enforcement—and corresponding "red" and "white" lines for fire and emergency services, respectively[3]—protects the citizenry but it can also encapsulate crisis responders within themselves and cut them off from the broader fabric of their communities.

One of the police officers we interviewed understands how camaraderie can turn into isolation. Perhaps she perceives this because she cannot be, by definition, part of the brotherhood: "It's a very secretive culture, and we don't like to share what goes on within the culture, and that certainly can be our demise when we don't do that." In terms set out by Maynard-Moody and Musheno (2000, 2003), the crisis responders we interviewed operate in accordance with a *citizen-agent narrative*. Our crisis responders act as agents of—on behalf of and in service to—the people, not as agents of the state. When asked, "To whom or what are you accountable?" each and every one invariably answered that it was to their teammates and to those they served. If they mentioned their employer at all, it was only after talking about their duty to citizens, and often sardonically and in reference to their administrative tasks: "I push a pencil, I put out fires. Not real ones, though. Not anymore." Serving people is their calling; serving the state is a job. Our "expert witnesses" to urban crisis response are thus similar to

Maynard-Moody and Musheno's (2003, p. 62): "Nearly all of the workers define themselves as advocates on a mission rather than bureaucrats implementing policy." However, unlike Maynard-Moody and Musheno's respondents, who included vocational rehabilitation counselors and middle school teachers, our respondents' professional lives are defined by chaos, crisis, and danger. We selected respondents based on the likelihood that they faced crisis as a matter of course. In sum, emotional labor is central to the exercise of discretion, and "how" our crisis responders exercise discretion is shaped by norms reinforced through traditions and symbols, including organizational hierarchy, uniforms, ranks, and team membership.

Summary

Discretion is unavoidable and not necessarily at odds with ethical behavior. And not all discretionary decisions are the same: Some decisions are small departures from the letter of the law; others are wholesale departures. The emotive skill is in finding the balance between the cost of exercising discretion, the degree of discretion to exercise, and the benefits of deviating from standard operating procedures. In the next chapter, our conclusions are synthesized. We further point toward the future and potential directions for more research and theory building on emotional labor in public service.

Notes

1. Incidentally, Illinois law is categorized as "officer's discretion" policy by the American Bar Association, rather than mandatory-arrest or pro-arrest. Whether Officer Preib and his partner perceived there to be discretion in this case or not, they in fact followed the letter of the law. Separately, another Chicago police officer told us that he thought arrests were mandatory as well. He related an incident in which the accused was a war veteran suffering from post-traumatic stress disorder and severe claustrophobia: "It took six guys to get him into lockup," a very small, enclosed space. The officers felt they had no choice but to make the arrest in accordance with the law, however. One responding officer recalled, "I really hated my job that night."

2. The academic administrators among us probably cannot help but fantasize how this scenario might play out in a faculty meeting, given what Jim Collins, best-selling author of *Good to Great* (2001), famously called academic faculty during his address to the annual conference of the information technology organization EDUCAUSE in 2009: "a thousand points of 'no.'" Although academic ranks are largely standard across institutions—assistant, associate, and full professor—they lack the "teeth" that ranks and titles possess in military and emergency service organizations. In other words, insubordination does not lead to penalties or dismissal in academia the way that it can in these organizations; the concept of insubordination itself lacks clear meaning in academia.

3. The "thin blue line" symbolizes the protective barrier composed of law enforcement officers to divide the citizenry from lawlessness. It is used to honor fallen officers, as recognized by the National Law Enforcement Officers' Memorial Fund (www. nleomf.org). Epolicesupply.com is a Massachusetts-based company that sells products under the Thin Line series, which uses blue, red, and white to symbolize police, fire, and emergency services, respectively; silver for corrections officers; yellow for private security; and green for federal protective services, including Border Patrol.

8

Reflections on the "Why," "How," and "What" of Emotional Labor

We engaged with this topic because we move through the world every day, just like everyone else, encountering other working people doing their jobs. But as scholars of work, we are at once among them and not of them. So we start asking questions. What do they do? How do they do it? And we have a particular interest in public service because it entails an added layer of expectation: "Not just a job, an adventure" as the old Peace Corps ads declared. Our interviewees confirmed this by referring consistently to their "duty" as more than just a paycheck.

We are also interested in public service because we believe John Rawls (1971) was right—we must take care of each other and there ought to be an entity representing collective interests because that next person in need might be one of us. We believe Thomas Hobbes (1651/1958) missed important aspects of human nature in his all-against-all wilderness. We believe that it is right and good that government in some form or another provides a harbor of refuge for those in need and that the harbor should be institutionalized and formalized rather than left to the voluntary charity of others. So, given an institutionalized government that manifests Rawlsian principles of collective care and action, who works there? What do they do, and how do they do it? At its base, this kind of work involves dealing with people, and commonly, it involves intense interpersonal relational work. Indeed, this is what we found in our earlier studies and what we confirm in this research.

Intense interpersonal work demands emotional labor. For pay. Emotions for sale. Emotion as duty. Early on, we thought that the invisibility of emotional labor explained the gender pay gap (Guy & Newman 2004). But only one type of emotional labor was examined in that study—care work—when, in fact, emotional labor takes many forms. Jobs demanding caring as a skill also happen to be female dominated, due in part to sex-role socialization that begins long before the individual enters the workforce. And female-dominated jobs are valued less and pay less than male-dominated jobs do, regardless of their emotional labor demands (Mastracci 2004). So, yes—care work is undervalued and women hold a disproportionate share of jobs that involve it. But no—it does not then follow that emotional labor explains the gender wage gap, because emotional labor is more than just care work. In the private sector, Hochschild (1983) studied jobs that demand intimidation and bullying and the effects that being intimidating had on workers. In public service, we studied jobs that demand extraordinary compassion and caring as well as jobs that required enforcing discipline and authority (Guy, Newman, & Mastracci 2008). All demand emotional labor. So we understand better what it is and why we are interested in studying it. But why do it? Why take a job that demands it?

Mainstream labor economics suggests that workers will take an emotionally demanding job if they are compensated enough to offset its rigors. Emotional laborers will agree to work in emotionally intense occupations if paid a risk premium, so to speak, like workers in other risky jobs are paid (Dorman 1996; Dorman & Hagstrom 1998; Garen 1988; Gunderson & Hyatt 2001; Leigh 1991; Meng & Smith 1999; Moore & Viscusi 1990; Olson 1981; Viscusi 1978, 1992). If those who work in emotionally intense jobs cannot demand a risk premium, it must be because they are not in a strong enough position to make demands. They can be replaced easily and/or they have few alternatives in the job market. Or, in economists' clumsy parlance, such workers face a highly elastic demand for their labor. On the other end of the ideological spectrum, Marxist theory claims that all work results in the alienation of labor—work alienates workers from themselves, resulting in an inauthentic self.

Our evidence suggests that neither theoretical frame is true. First, pay in public service jobs tends to be lower than in similar occupations in the private sector (Guy & Newman 2004; Guy et al. 2008). This contradicts the claim that a risk premium accompanies these jobs. Second, plenty of public servants in such jobs are highly educated professionals who would enjoy a range of options in the labor market (Guy et al. 2008). This undermines the claim relating to demand elasticity. Finally, not only are such workers able to avoid alienation and inauthenticity (Lopez 2006), but many public servants choose these jobs and feel rewarded for their efforts, often because of the emotional labor demands (Guy et al. 2008).

Now, we understand better who the people are who serve others and why they do what they do—but *how* do they do what they do? We embarked on this journey to discover *how* public servants performed emotional labor, how they made decisions under pressure, how they found the stamina to return the next day and the next to do it all over again. [1] We chose those who serve in the most extreme circumstances because for each of their actions, there is no "do-over." They must act quickly, invoking all of their emotive strengths in a matter of minutes, if not seconds. Their performance is a compressed, condensed version of emotional labor as it is performed in calmer public service jobs every day.

Reflections on the "What" of Emotional Labor

So what have we learned and what does it mean? First, we have long argued the importance of recognizing emotional labor. Emerging research in this area underscores its crucial importance. It is a "comes with" for all jobs where public servant meets citizen. Not only are cognitive skills essential; emotive skills are as well. If we are to hire, train, develop, and evaluate workers on the basis of their performance, we must include consideration of the whole job, not just its cognitive aspects. Workers must be able to suppress, control, or elicit their own and others' emotions as the job demands. In other words, their capacity to engage in, and their efficacy in, exerting emotional labor is essential to job performance.

Second, we challenged mainstream management theory, proverbs, and principles, because we are still left with a fairly barren landscape when it comes to explaining emotional labor in public service. We are still stuck with an image of work forged during the industrial age by management scientists blind to the human processes by which work gets done. Only scholarship at the fringes has exposed the problems of management dictating orders from higher levels in the organization to lower levels as though hierarchical position equals degree of expertise. In contrast, our emphasis on crisis responders at the scene of an incident means that we place emotional labor expertise at the front lines, not farther up the hierarchy. Despite poststructuralist inroads into scholarship on organizations (Acker 1990, 1992; also see research on "street-level bureaucracy"), placing expertise at the front lines contradicts public management orthodoxy rooted in the work of Weber (1922/1997).

Our critique of mainstream scholarship on governance flows directly from the paradigm set forth by Mary Parker Follett, who articulated an alternative to patriarchal, dictatorial management. Hers is a democratic, representative, empowering, interactive relationship that relies heavily on emotional labor. Without calling it so, Follett advises managers to communicate on an emotional level in order to accomplish organizational objectives (Follett 1926/1997, 53; emphasis supplied):

> You cannot get people to do things most satisfactorily by ordering them or exhorting them . . . even reasoning with them, even convincing them intellectually, may not be enough . . . business administration, industrial

organization, should build up certain habit-patterns, that is, certain mental attitudes. . . . [W]e have to do three things: (1) build up certain attitudes; (2) provide for the release of these attitudes; [and] (3) augment the released response as it is being carried out.

Tapping into one's own and others' "mental attitudes" is at the heart of emotion work. Unlike her contemporaries, Follett observes how and explains why dictating orders down through the hierarchy will not work well, nor will reason or persuasion at a purely cognitive level. Follett understands the importance of addressing the emotional realm in order to change worker behavior. Follett's effective manager is one who reaches goals by obtaining buy-in and facilitating the success of employees rather than by unilateral commands.

Drawing and redrawing organizational charts, writing and rewriting organizational rules, and reviewing and revising procedures in an effort to perfect them are only half of management's job. Thinking that this is sufficient to guarantee particular outcomes is to treat human processes like computer code. In computer programming, getting the zeroes and ones right will, indeed, produce a particular outcome. Every time. In the management of people, it is arguable whether such things as perfectly clear rules and procedures even exist, much less whether they can ensure optimal outcomes time after time. People were not cogs in the industrial age when early management literature was written any more than they are zeroes and ones during the information age.

The top-down nature of management and administration is inherently patriarchal. Deconstructing orthodox public administration and questioning its patriarchal habits of mind invite the creation of a counterpoint, which is exactly what Mary Parker Follett presented in 1926, contemporaneously alongside *en vogue* scientific management ideals of Frederick Taylor (1911/1997), Henry Ford, and the posthumously published translations of Max Weber (1922/1997). We, too, seek to fracture the scholarship orthodoxy by placing emotional labor front and center in our investigation into practice, examining how it is done on the front lines. Ours is an argument that will need to be repeated as long as mainstream scholarship insists on reproducing positivist ideals by focusing on only what can be counted, by seeing only what is under the lamppost.

Deirdre McCloskey characterizes acontextual modeling of human behavior as games played by boys in the sandbox. Whatever rules and assumptions are made in the sandbox may apply quite well there, but outside—in the real world—the assumptions have no meaning. And yet the boys in the sandbox—in our case, mainstream theory—take their assumption-ridden, flawed results as truth: "They are so earnest in their play, so full of confidence and life, so sure that what they are playing is reality" (McCloskey 1996, p. 13). Likewise, most research on management and governance is done earnestly, confident that it reflects reality outside the sandbox. In Chapter 2, we revisited our argument that orthodox public administration scholarship still fails to "see" emotional labor because the sandbox games remain so popular, so seductive.

In the third chapter, we gave employers a job: prepare your employees for emotional labor demands and equip them with the skills and resources for managing their own and others' emotions as their work situations demand. Emotion work is intense and pays dividends to workers in the form of giving meaning to their workday and leaving them with a feeling that their work matters and that it makes a difference in people's lives. Screening recruits to make sure that they are confident in their emotional skills and self-aware of their own feelings is an important component of the hiring process. This means that job candidates who are in touch with their own feelings and are able to articulate them are better equipped to perform emotion work and to deal with its consequences.

Once on the job, training sessions that alert workers to normal emotional demands help sensitize them to the emotive dimension of their work. Discussions of how to deal with the emotional trappings of the job serve to develop awareness and help them take proactive steps to anticipate and deal with their encounters and the recollections that follow. For example, a flight nurse who treats accident victims as they are being flown by helicopter to treatment centers told us that rookie responders often are surprised at the intensity of their emotional response during or after a call (Liska 2010). Had they known to anticipate these feelings, they would know that what they are experiencing is normal. Knowing this in advance of the experience prevents their thinking that they "can't handle" the job and encourages them to discuss these feelings with coworkers.

There are two strategies responders told us about that help them deal with the consequences of intense emotional labor. These are self-care plans, a preventive strategy, and critical incident stress management, which is episodic and done after the fact on an as-needed basis. Self-care plans have the intention of keeping workers continuously alert to the fact that they have a life and goals separate from their work experience. They are required to set stretch goals for themselves that may range from weight control to travel to hobbies to lifestyle changes. Whatever these goals are, they differ from job duties. To ensure that workers take their plan seriously, their supervisor evaluates them on whether they achieved their annual personal goals at the same time that they are evaluated on their annual work performance.

Critical incident stress management usually consists of debriefings either requested by workers who have experienced an emotionally intense encounter or required by the employer when it is obvious that workers have leftover issues from an encounter. A counselor who is skilled in facilitating discussion of episodic events in a group setting is called in to guide the session. An alternative to this strategy is regularly scheduled meetings where workers discuss problematic cases or events. The objective for episodic or regularly scheduled discussions is for workers to air their experiences in a safe, knowing environment among coworkers who have similar experiences.

In emotion work, the highs are high and the lows can be very low. Employers and supervisors need to acknowledge the highs and anticipate the lows. They can do this by providing mechanisms that celebrate the upside while not ignoring the downside and leaving individuals to rebound on their own. In the absence of strategies for coping with haunting recollections long after the job is done, workers too often turn "crispy," engaging in dysfunctional behaviors, losing interest in their work, and seeking work elsewhere. Losing trained, competent workers is expensive and, with forethought, avoidable.

We approached various facets and faces of crisis response by featuring different types of work: the messenger, the hero, the supervisor, the ones who made mistakes, the ones who run toward the burning building while citizens run away, the ones who have seen it all. The messengers are public information officers (PIOs). They may not have experienced the crisis directly, but they must convey information with the level of detail as if they had. They make and manage meanings, establish trust and competence, and control the message. They are the face of the agency and, as such, must match their own affect to the situation. They must control their own emotion on behalf of the entire organization, all the while conveying accurate and precise information. Theirs is a unique role in crisis response.

In Chapters 5, 6, and 7, we addressed three important dimensions of governance that are directly implicated in the exercise of emotional labor: accountability, legitimacy, and discretion. Accountability and responsiveness take on new meanings in the emotionally intense context of crisis response. Well-planned procedures and standing orders are designed to make decision making almost automatic. But no prescribed plans can cover all the exigencies of a crisis situation. Responders pair their cognitive knowledge with their own emotional state as well as that of those around them. Like doing double duty, this pairing is a skill that research shows is developed over time, with more experienced workers able to do a better job of it than rookies.

Legitimacy in a highly charged environment relates to the PIO's burden to represent the agency, framing its message and delivering it in a way that instills confidence and resonates with listeners. It also relates to the work of each public servant because those who meet the public are the face of the agency and of government in general. Chapter 6 investigated factors related to the legitimacy of such representation. How are legitimacy and trust earned? One significant factor turned out to be the uniforms and regalia worn by crisis responders and the symbols and rituals used to convey authority. Uniforms take away the individual characteristics of workers and turn them into "generic" responders. This has the effect of emphasizing the authority of the state while masking demographic differences. The workers *become* their role, rather than a person playing the role.

There remains much to be learned about demographic representativeness and the exercise of emotional labor. Although it may be fair to assume that a worker and a citizen of similar background and culture can reach consensus faster than if they look and live differently from each another, this dynamic has yet to be studied. From the words of the young woman firefighter who met resistance not only from fellow firefighters but also from the citizen she was aiding, it is clear that expectations about rescuers make a difference in the trust that citizens and sometimes coworkers have. When workers do not look like what the citizen expects, extra effort—and emotional control—are required.

The role of the uniform came up again in Chapter 7's discussion of discretion, where it was related to accountability, legitimacy, and trust. Who is "allowed" to exercise discretion when the stakes are as high as they are in crisis response, and how is it done? Rank and hierarchy are significant determinants of who is authorized to exercise discretion in emotionally intense incidents. And the answer to "how" emotional labor is exercised in discretionary decision making turned out to be "very carefully," with acute awareness of consequences and desired outcomes.

Further Reflections

At this point, it is appropriate to draw back from crisis responders as one type of public servant and discuss public servants and emotional labor in general. As we explained in the first chapter, we focused on crisis responders as a convenience because their work provides a compressed version of public service engagements with citizens more generally. This methodological choice allowed us to aim the magnifying glass at decision making and performance under acute emotive stress, not unlike Carole Gilligan's (1982) approach to studying moral decision making by focusing on women faced with the decision whether or not to abort a pregnancy.

Whether public servants come in contact with citizens over a reception desk, at the tax assessor's office, at a zoning hearing, or in a crisis, emotional labor will be required. While the upside to emotion work is more prevalent, there is a downside. All public servants would do well to have at their disposal self-care plans and critical incident stress management in some form, even though most of them operate in an atmosphere of meetings and emails and not one of victims and crises. Most of them do not operate in organizations that are structured according to rank, regalia, and a strong command-and-control hierarchy. Such structure is needed in crisis response, but is usually not appropriate in other public service organizations.

The silence-to-violence cycle described by Patterson, Grenny, McMillan, & Switzler (2002) provides a parallel, although exaggerated, understanding of how and why there are benefits to training and development in regard to emotional labor skills. As creators of *Crucial Conversations*, Patterson and his colleagues describe a silence-to-violence cycle that starts with ignoring felt emotions out of a desire to remain professional or appear in control. But avoiding crucial conversations and suppressing emotions have corrosive effects. Workers start making mistakes that they would otherwise not make because the suppression of emotion—the deleterious form of emotional labor—takes its toll and impedes cognitive function, introducing performance-related concerns. The silence ends and violence emerges with fury, whether the violence manifests as physical or emotional. Meanings are made and interpreted through a haze of long-suppressed emotions—through the haze of minds impaired by prolonged emotional suppression. Sometimes the crucial conversation happens too late. The damage is done. Good people quit or self-destruct. They become crispy. Good workers begin to falter over time and are let go for poor performance. Teams with potential dissolve.

Whose "fault" is it? Are failed relationships the fault of those choosing silence, avoiding crucial conversations in an effort to maintain composure or save face? Or are they the fault of those similarly suffering the effects of emotional suppression but resorting to confrontational means out of frustration with the silence, the order of things? Or rather, are they the responsibility of the employer? Who should be aware of the emotional labor demands on workers and the effects of not attending to them? We argue that it is everyone's responsibility, but the strategies must exist in the organization, designed by the employer just as training is provided to enhance performance of technical skills.

We heard from organizations that have institutionalized self-care plans, but even the most vigilant ones can grow complacent. Even organizations that are aware of the presence and importance of emotional labor must continuously engage in training and retraining, for even the best teams can suffer the silence of conversations ignored, of emotional labor demands unacknowledged. Who, then, decides what a "crucial" conversation is? Who decides what constitutes problematic silence and what is simply professionalism?

Another organizational responsibility is to negotiate and renegotiate norms within which employees can do their best work. It is the rare organization that can afford a policy of silence and avoid crucial conversations. These are questions that rise to the level of organizational operations and for which this book provides a basis for further inquiry.

There are additional questions whose answers would make it easier to understand the nuances of emotional labor. Although outside the scope of this book, they are pertinent to the subject and invite attention. For instance, we know that emotional labor is an important component of leadership, but we do not know much about the gradations involved, how they are exercised, and what the trigger points are for those in leadership positions (Newman, Guy, & Mastracci 2009). We know that public service motivation and emotion work are not directly related but that compassion and emotion work are (Hsieh 2009). We have a hunch that it is the upside of emotional labor that reinforces compassion and vice versa. How public service motivation factors into the equation remains to be learned.

The constructs of emotional intelligence and emotional labor have yet to be reconciled (ibid.). In theory, the former is the substrate upon which the performance of emotional labor depends. This is analogous to cognition, where intelligence is the substrate upon which cognitive achievement depends. In other words, if one scores high on emotional intelligence, one should score high in the performance of emotion work. This connection has yet to be verified, however. All in all, public administration scholarship is on the cusp of change, assuming that it moves to embrace emotion work along with cognitive work. To do so will acknowledge the full human being in the workplace, rather than only half the person. To do so will transform public administration theory into public service theory.

The implications for emotional labor in public service are thus: Through selective recruitment of applicants who are technically skilled *and* emotionally self-aware, the workforce is better equipped to deliver public services. Training and development that targets worker knowledge about emotional labor and the feelings that are normal in such work will advance the performance of emotion work and proactively reduce its downside. Emotional labor is a skill. It can be learned and developed. Management can provide training that can improve workers' job performance and mitigate the negative effects of emotional labor on their lives outside of work. This is possible—whether or not you work on the razor's edge.

Note

1. Addressing these issues was suggested by Lizette Michael, formerly of the University of Toronto.

Appendix A
Evidentiary Proceedings

We chose emergency response based on the high likelihood of its practitioners to exert emotional labor in intense interpersonal situations and to be vulnerable to primary and secondary traumatic stress (Figley 1994; Stamm 2008). Workers in the sample included police officers, firefighters, emergency medical technicians, crisis hotline workers, sexual assault nurse examiners, trauma nurse managers, medical examiners, public hospital administrators, and domestic violence and victim assistance workers. Patterns and trends in their perceptions of their own performance, role expectations, accountability, responsiveness, and discretion were revealed through textual interpretation of interview transcripts.

Forty-three respondents participated in this project. Fourteen interviews in Chicago[1] were conducted between February 25 and August 23, 2010; seven interviews in Denver took place from June 14 through 28, 2010; and interviews of twenty-two respondents in Miami took place between October 29, 2009, and March 1, 2010. In total, more than forty-three hours of interview time was logged by the researchers. Respondents were selected strictly on the basis of job function—that is, whether they currently serve or ever served as first responders.

The authors live in Chicago, Denver, and Miami, respectively, and each selected interviewees in those metropolitan areas. Some initial contacts were cold calls; others were the product of referrals (i.e., "snowball sampling"). In all, this project is based on the expertise of experienced crisis responders who have responded to hundreds of emergencies, including the September 11, 2001, attack on the World Trade Center in New York City, Hurricane Andrew in south Florida in 1992, Hurricane Katrina in New Orleans in 2005, the Haiti earthquake in 2010, and the Columbine school shootings in 1999. Jurisdictions represented by our study participants include the following:[2]

- Arvada (Colorado) Police Department
- Chicago Fire Department
- Chicago Police Department
- City of Chicago, Illinois
- City/County of Denver, Colorado
- City of Miami, Florida
- City of Miami, Florida Division of Emergency Management
- Jackson Memorial Hospital (Miami, Florida)
- Jefferson County, Colorado
- Medical Examiner Department, Miami-Dade County, Florida
- Miami-Dade County, Florida
- Miami-Dade Fire Rescue Department, Florida
- Miami Police Department
- Pleasantview, Illinois Fire Protection District
- Safe House Denver, Denver, Colorado
- State of Illinois Police
- United States Coast Guard, Florida
- Westminster (Colorado) Police Department

Study participants were informed of the risks and benefits of participation in accordance with the standards of each author's Institutional Review Board.[3] Participants were interviewed according to our interview protocol (see Appendix B), which was developed in consultation with a practicing crisis responder from one of the study sites. Researchers interviewed respondents at their places of work in order to maintain the focus on the respondent and his or her work, unless participants chose to be interviewed elsewhere. We interviewed respondents to elicit stories about their experiences. At the outset, we made the following assumptions:

- Crisis responders have engaged in emotional labor.
- When asked, they can articulate it.
- Stories of extreme incidents—the worst, the most chaotic, etc.—generate memories of how they shut out the chaos and responded to crisis (i.e., *how* they engaged in emotional labor).
- Stories of crisis response demonstrate the objective reality of emotional labor.
- Crisis responders' tacit knowledge of how to do emotional labor can be made explicit via interview, transcription, and analysis of their stories.

Interviews were recorded and lasted about an hour each. The recordings were transcribed by Nottingham Transcription Studio in Orlando, Florida.

Transcription documents produced the "word data" (Yanow & Schwartz-Shea 2006, p. xix) upon which our results were based. Transcript analysis was also facilitated by use of the qualitative data analysis software package ATLAS.ti. We allowed constructs to emerge from respondents' observations and analyzed constructs in order to find meanings. Using their voices as expert testimony, we examined patterns of behavior and decision making in crisis response from the ground up, rather than imposing frameworks onto their narratives from the top down. As such, we make no claims with respect to random sampling of study participants or universal representation of their narratives because, in this study, "concepts are embedded within a literature . . . the attempt to specify them once and for all as universal constructs violates interpretive presuppositions about the historical locatedness of scholars and actors" (ibid., p. xvii).

Our chief method in this study was discourse analysis. The veracity of our claims is based not on statistical significance, but rather on the rigor and logic of our argument, given the evidence, and by addressing plausible alternative explanations. Discourse analysis is not a common approach to analysis in public administration research, but it suits the study of emotional labor because emotional labor itself resists quantification and is not easily detected "on the basis of external observation *alone*" (ibid., p. xviii). In fact, if it is done right, an external observer should not be able to detect it at all. Its study, therefore, required the use of appropriate methodology:

> To claim that something is knowable entails a related claim in regard to its "reality status." Epistemological and ontological claims are mutually implicating—*and* they implicate methodological choices. If one claims that a door is objectively real (its existence is independent of, and external to, the observer) and that it is knowable through external ("objective") observation, then positivism's scientific method is a reasonable methodological procedure to choose for establishing and supporting truth claims emerging from research into some aspect of that door. If one can't claim knowledge of an organization or a community on the basis of external observation *alone*, then one needs a different methodology and different methods for producing and supporting knowledge claims. (ibid., p. xviii, emphasis original)

To ensure the rigor of the construct-development process, we three authors met—either in person or via teleconference—once a month over the life of this project. One of us maintained a reflexive journal used in the interpretive analysis process, and we have remained in touch with at least some of our respondents for follow-up and feedback. Finally, our use of a single interview protocol in three different settings and executed by three different researchers approximates triangulation found in multiple-methods research.

Notes

1. In Chicago, fourteen people were interviewed and two asked to be removed from consideration, netting twelve usable interviews and ten transcripts (two declined to be recorded). The recruitment process stopped as a pattern of refusals became apparent. Refusals—either to participate or be recorded—were not random, and they resulted in an imbalance of voices from fire services vis-à-vis law enforcement in Chicago. It is likely that the refusals stemmed from deepening distrust between the superintendent of police and the rank and file. In February 2009, members of the Chicago Lodge #7 of the Fraternal Order of Police (FOP) gave a vote of "no confidence" to Superintendent Jody Weis. A series of events—including the murders of three uniformed officers—from 2009 through the summer of 2010 culminated in a public spat between the union and the superintendent in the editorial pages of the Chicago *Sun-Times* and then an unprecedented protest against the superintendent on September 15, 2010, during which the membership demanded his resignation. On the eve of the protest, FOP Chicago Lodge president Mark Donahue told reporters, "He came in with three or four advisors from outside the department, he had no experience with dealing with municipal law enforcement in his career, and he has failed to listen to men and women within the police department, *he'd rather take the recommendations of academics*" (Donahue 2010, emphasis supplied). And the following is a recap of the protest in the union's October 2010 newsletter (Donahue 2010, p. 2, emphasis supplied):

> On top of the no confidence vote taken by the membership in February 2009 and the superintendent's factually devoid tirade in the *Sun-Times*, he left no doubt that he needs to go. Not only from a Law Enforcement perspective, but from a community protection perspective and even a Labor perspective (in large part due to his article), he has proven his inability to listen to those around him (*preferring to listen to the academics*) and his incompetence in securing his personnel and the citizens in this City from crime.

The point is that 2009–2010 was no climate for academic research involving the Chicago Police Department. We do not know to which academics the union refers or on what topics they may have advised the superintendent. All we know is that it became increasingly difficult and then impossible to engage members of the Chicago police in this research project, resulting in their comparatively lesser representation at that study site, relative to fire and emergency services.

2. This list is incomplete in order to protect the anonymity and confidentiality of study participants from smaller offices or jurisdictions.

3. Florida International University Institutional Review Board (IRB) protocol #210677; University of Colorado Denver IRB protocol #09–0806; and University of Illinois at Chicago IRB protocol #2009–0670.

Appendix B
Interview Protocol

1. When someone asks you to describe your job, what do you usually say?
2. In your line of work, do you feel a certain responsibility toward a particular group?
    a. If so, who or what?
3. Have you ever had an incident where your abilities or credibility was questioned? For instance, has anyone ever said to you:
    • Do you have any idea what I'm going through?
    • Aren't you a little young/old to be doing this?
    • Do you have any idea what you're doing?
    • You don't look/sound like a _____.
    a. What happened?
    b. What did you do?
4. Have you ever had an incident when you had to bend or break the rules (think entirely outside the box, something came out of left field, etc.)?—when you had to suddenly change course, readjust, or depart from standard operating procedure?
    a. What happened?
    b. What did you do?
5. Have you ever suffered your own crisis of confidence?
    a. What happened?
    b. What did you do?
6. Have you ever had a completely chaotic incident when it was up to you (there was no one else to turn to) to reestablish control? Alternatively, have you ever been called in to help someone else handle an incident?
    a. What happened?
    b. What did you do?

7. Is there a particular incident that sticks out in your mind when everything went wrong?
   a. What happened?
   b. What did you do?
   c. What was the fallout?
   d. What role, if any, does this case play in the way you do your job now?
8. Is there a particular incident that sticks out in your mind when everything went right?
   a. What happened?
   b. What did you do?
   c. What was the fallout?
   d. What role, if any, does this case play in the way you do your job now?

References

Acker, J. (1990). Hierarchies, jobs, bodies: A theory of gendered organizations. *Gender & Society*, 4, 139–158.

———. (1992). From sex roles to gendered institutions. *Contemporary Sociology*, 21, 565–569.

Adair, B. (2002). Ten years ago, her angry plea got hurricane aid moving. *St. Petersburg Times*, August 20. www.sptimes.com/2002/webspecials02/andrew/day3/story1.shtml.

Adams, G.B., Balfour, D.L., & Reed, G.E. (2006). Abu Ghraib, administrative evil, and moral inversion: The value of "putting cruelty first." *Public Administration Review*, 66, 680–693.

Alonso, P., & Lewis, G.B. (2001). Public service motivation and job performance. *The American Review of Public Administration*, 31, 363–380.

American Bar Association (ABA) Commission on Domestic Violence. (2007). Domestic violence arrest policies by state. November. www.abanet.org/domviol.

Ashforth, B.E., & Humphrey, R.H. (1993). Emotional labor in service roles: The influence of identity. *Academy of Management Review*, 18, 88–115.

Banks, S.P. (1995). *Multicultural Public Relations: A Social-Interpretive Approach*. Thousand Oaks, CA: Sage.

Bardach, E., & Lesser, C. (1996). Accountability in human services collaborative: For what? To whom? *Journal of Public Administration Research and Theory*, 6, 197–224.

Battaglio, R., & Condrey, S. (2009). Reforming public management: Analyzing the impact of public service reform on organizational and managerial trust. *Journal of Public Administration Research and Theory*, 19, 689–707.

Beck, U. (1992). *Risk Society: Towards a New Modernity*. London: Sage.

Berge, D. (1990). *The First 24 Hours: A Comprehensive Guide to Successful Crisis Communications*. Cambridge, MA: Basil Blackwell.

Berman, E.M., & West, J.P. (2008). Managing emotional intelligence in U.S. cities: A study of social skills among public managers. *Public Administration Review*, 68, 742–758.

Berry, S. (1999). We have a problem . . . call the press! *Public Management*, 81, 4–9.

Bhave, D.P., & Glomb, T.M. (2009). Emotional labour demands, wages and gender: A within-person, between-jobs study. *Journal of Occupational and Organizational Psychology*, 82, 683–707.

Birnbaum, D.W. (1983). Preschoolers' stereotypes about sex differences in emotionality: A reaffirmation. *Journal of Genetic Psychology*, 143, 139–140.

Blumberg, S.K. (1981). Seven decades of public administration: A tribute to Luther Gulick. *Public Administration Review*, 41, 245–248.

Blumenberg, E. (2002). On the way to work: Welfare participants and barriers to employment. *Economic Development Quarterly*, 16, 314–325.

Brehm, J., & Gates, S. (1997). *Working, Shirking, and Sabotage: Bureaucratic Response to a Democratic Public*. Ann Arbor: University of Michigan Press.

Brodkin, E.Z. (2007). Bureaucracy redux: Management reformism and the welfare state. *Journal of Public Administration Research and Theory*, 17, 1–17.

Brody, L.R. (1985). Gender differences in emotional development: A review of theories and research. *Journal of Personality*, 53, 102–149.

Brody, L.R., & Hall, J.A. (2008). Gender and emotion in context. In *Handbook of Emotions*, 3rd ed., ed. M. Lewis & J. Haviland-Jones. New York: Guilford.

Brunacini, A. (1985). *Fire Command, National Fire Protection Association*. Quincy, MA: National Fire Protection Association.

Bryan, J.B. (2005). Have the 1996 welfare reforms and expansion of the earned income tax credit eliminated the need for a basic income guarantee in the U.S.? *Review of Social Economy*, 63, 595–611.

Burke, L.A., & Miller, M.K. (1999). Taking the mystery out of intuitive decision making. *Academy of Management Executive*, 13, 91–99.

Burkhart, F.N. (1991). *Media, Emergency Warnings, and Citizen Response*. Boulder CO: Westview Press.

Carey, B. (2009). Army will train soldiers to cope with emotions: Changing the culture. *New York Times*, August 18, pp. A1, A3.

Carmeli, A. (2003). The relationship between emotional intelligence and work attitudes, behavior and outcomes: An examination among senior managers. *Journal of Managerial Psychology*, 18, 788–813.

CBS/Associated Press. (2010). Last man safely reaches surface in Chile. October 13. www.cbsnews.com/stories/2010/10/13/world/main6955701.shtml?tag=cbsContent;cbsCarousel.

Collins, J. (2001). *Good to Great: Why Some Companies Make the Leap to Greatness and Others Don't*. New York: Harper Collins.

Comfort, L.K. (1988). Synthesis in disaster management: Linking reason with action in learning systems. In *Managing Disaster: Strategies and Policy Perspectives*, ed. L.K. Comfort. Durham, NC: Duke University Press.

———. (1989). The San Salvador earthquake. In *Coping with Crises: The Management of Disasters, Riots, and Terrorism,* ed. U. Rosenthal, M.T. Charles, & P.T. Hart. Springfield, IL: Charles C. Thomas.

———. (2002). Rethinking security: Organizational fragility in extreme events. *Public Administration Review*, 62, 98–107.

Comfort, L.K., & Cahill, A.G. (1988). Increasing problem-solving capacity between organizations: The role of information in managing the May 31, 1985, tornado disaster in western Pennsylvania. In *Managing Disaster: Strategies and Policy Perspectives*, ed. L.K. Comfort. Durham, NC: Duke University Press.

Comfort, L.K., Ko, K., & Zagorecki, A. (2004). Coordination in rapidly evolving disaster response systems: The role of information. *American Behavioral Scientist*, 48, 295–313.

Coombs, W.T. (1999). *Ongoing Crisis Communication: Planning, Managing, and Responding.* Thousand Oaks, CA: Sage.

Coursey, D.H., & Pandey, S.K. (2007). Public service motivation measurement: Testing an abridged version of Perry's proposed scale. *Administration and Society,* 39, 547–568.

Crable, R.E., & Vibbert, S.L. (1986). *Public Relations as Communication Management.* Edina, MN: Bellwether.

Crichton, M.T., Flin, R., & Rattray, W.A.R. (2000). Training decision makers: Tactical decision games. *Journal of Contingencies and Crisis Management,* 8, 208–217.

Cropp, F., & Pincus, J.D. (2001). The mystery of public relations: Unraveling its past, unmasking its future. In *Handbook of Public Relations,* ed. R.L. Heath. Thousand Oaks, CA: Sage.

Cross, C.L., & Ashley, L. (2004). Police trauma and addiction: Coping with the dangers of the job. *FBI Law Enforcement Bulletin,* 73, 24–32.

Crump, J.R. (2003). The end of public housing as we know it: Public housing policy, labor regulation and the U.S. city. *International Journal of Urban and Regional Research,* 27, 179–187.

D'Aprix, R. (1988). Communication as process: The manager's view. In *Handbook of Organizational Communication,* ed. G.M. Goldhaber & G.A. Barnett. Norwood, NJ: Ablex Press.

Daugherty, E.L. (2001). Public relations and social responsibility. In *Handbook of Public Relations,* ed. R.L. Heath. Thousand Oaks, CA: Sage.

Day, P., & Klein, R. (1987). *Accountabilities: Five Public Services.* London: Tavistock.

Denhardt, J.V., & Denhardt, R.B. (2005). *The Dance of Leadership: The Art of Leading in Business, Government, and Society.* Armonk, NY: M.E. Sharpe.

Dobel, J. (1990). Integrity in public service. *Public Administration Review,* 50(2), 354–366.

Donahue, M. (2010). President's Report. FOP News, October. www.chicagofop.org/news/2010/102010news.pdf.

Dorman, P. (1996). *Markets and Mortality: Economics, Dangerous Work and the Value of Human Life.* Cambridge, UK: Cambridge University Press.

Dorman, P., & Hagstrom, P. (1998). Wage compensation for dangerous work, revisited. *Industrial and Labor Relations Review,* 52, 116–135.

Dozier, D.M. (1992). The organizational roles of communications and public relations practitioners. In *Excellence in Public Relations and Communication Management,* ed. J.E. Grunig. Hillsdale, NJ: Lawrence Erlbaum.

Drabek, T.E. (1986). *Human System Responses to Disaster: An Inventory of Sociological Findings.* New York: Springer-Verlag.

Dror, Y. (1988). Decision making under disaster conditions. In *Managing Disaster: Strategies and Policy Perspectives,* ed. L.K. Comfort. Durham, NC: Duke University Press.

Dubnick, M.J., & Romzek, B.S. (1993). Accountability and the centrality of expectations. In *Research in Public Administration,* ed. J.M. Perry. Greenwich, CT: JAI Press.

Dunn, B.D., Billotti, D., Murphy, V., & Dalgleish, T. (2009). The consequences of effortful emotion regulation when processing distressing material: A comparison of suppression and acceptance. *Behaviour Research and Therapy,* 47, 761–773.

Eden, D. (1991). Applying impression management to create productive self-fulfilling prophecy at work. In *Applied Impression Management: How Image-Making Affects Managerial Decisions*, ed. R.A. Giacaione & P. Rosenfeld. Newbury Park, CA: Sage.

Ehling, W.P. (1992). Estimating the value of public relations and communication to an organization. In *Excellence in Public Relations and Communication Management*, ed. J.E. Grunig. Hillsdale, NJ: Lawrence Erlbaum.

Ekman, P. (1973). Cross culture studies of facial expressions. In *Darwin and Facial Expression: A Century of Research in Review*, ed. P. Ekman. New York: Academic Press.

Evans, P., Rueschemeyer, D., & Skocpol, T. (1985). *Bringing the State Back In*. New York: Cambridge University Press.

Falkheimer, J., & Heide, M. (2006). Multicultural crisis communication: Toward a social constructionist perspective. *Journal of Contingencies and Crisis Management*, 14, 180–189.

Figley, C.R. (1994). Post-traumatic stress disorder in family psychologists. In *Family Psychology and Systems Therapy: A Handbook,* ed. R.H. Mikesell, D. Lusterman, & S.H. McDaniel, pp. 571–584. Washington, DC: American Psychological Association.

Finer, H. (1941). Administrative responsibility in democratic government. *Public Administration Review*, 1, 335–350.

Foa, E.B., Cahill, S.P., Boscarino, J.A., Hobfoll, S.E., Lahad, M., McNally, R.J., & Solomon, Z. (2005). Social, psychological, and psychiatric interventions following terrorist attacks: Recommendations for practice and research. *Neuropsychopharmacology*, 30, 1806–1817.

Follett, M.P. (1926/1997). The giving of orders. In *Classics of Public Administration*, 4th ed., ed. J.M. Shafritz & A.C. Hyde, pp. 53–60. Fort Worth, TX: Harcourt Brace.

Franklin, J. (2010). Chilean miners get media training to prepare for life above ground. *Guardian UK*, September 22. www.guardian.co.uk/world/2010/sep/22/chilean-miners-media-training.

Frederickson, H.G., & Hart, D.K. (1985). The public service and the patriotism of benevolence. *Public Administration Review*, 45, 547–553.

Friedman, M. (1962). *Capitalism and Freedom*. Chicago: University of Chicago Press.

Friedrich, C.J. (1940). Public policy and the nature of administrative responsibility. In *Public Policy: A Yearbook of the Graduate School of Public Administration*, ed. C.J. Friedrich & E.S. Mason. Cambridge, MA: Harvard University Press.

Frye, V., Haviland, M., & Rajah, V. (2007). Dual arrest and other unintended consequences of mandatory arrest in New York City. *Journal of Family Violence*, 22, 397–405.

Gabris, G.T., & Simo, G. (1995). Public sector motivation as an independent variable affecting career decisions. *Public Personnel Management*, 24, 33–51.

Garen, J. (1988). Compensating wage differentials and the endogeneity of job riskiness. *Review of Economics and Statistics*, 70, 9–16.

Garnett, J.L. (1992). *Communicating for Results in Government. A Strategic Approach for Public Managers*. San Francisco: Jossey-Bass.

Garnett, J.L., & Kouzmin, A. (2007). Communicating throughout Katrina: Competing and complementary conceptual lenses on crisis communication. *Public Administration Review,* S171–188.

Gilligan, C. (1982). *In a Different Voice: Psychological Theory and Women's Development.* Cambridge, MA: Harvard University Press.

Goffman, E. (1981). *Forms of Talk.* Philadelphia: University of Pennsylvania Press.

Goleman, D. (2006). *Emotional Intelligence: Why It Can Matter More Than IQ,* 10th Anniversary Ed. New York: Bantam Books.

Goss, C. (2005). Mental health aftermath of simulated attacks. *Law & Order,* 53, 48–55.

Gross, J.J., & Thompson, R.A. (2007). Emotion regulation: Conceptual foundations. In *Handbook of Emotion Regulation,* ed. J.J. Gross. New York: Guilford Press.

Grunig, L.A., Grunig, J.E., & Dozier, D.M. (2002). *Excellent Public Relations and Effective Organizations: A Study of Communication Management in Three Countries.* Mahwah, NJ: Lawrence Erlbaum.

Grunig, L.A., Grunig, J.E., & Ehling, W.P. (1992). What is an effective organization? In *Excellence in Public Relations and Communication Management,* ed. J.E. Grunig. Hillsdale, NJ: Lawrence Erlbaum.

Grunig, J.E., & Hunt, T. (1984). *Managing Public Relations.* New York: Harper & Row.

Gunderson, M.K., & Hyatt, D. (2001). Workplace risk and wages: Evidence from alternative models. *Canadian Journal of Economics,* 34, 377–395.

Guy, M.E. (1985). *Professionals in Organizations: Debunking a Myth.* New York: Praeger.

Guy, M.E., & Newman, M.A. (2004). Women's jobs, men's jobs: Sex segregation and emotional labor. *Public Administration Review,* 64(3), 289–298.

Guy, M.E., Newman, M.A., & Mastracci, S.H. (2008). *Emotional Labor: Putting the Service in Public Service.* Armonk, NY: M.E. Sharpe.

Haise, C.L., & Rucker, M. (2003). The flight attendant uniform: Effects of selected variables on flight attendant image, uniform preferences and employee satisfaction. *Social Behavior and Personality,* 31, 565–576.

Hall, E.T. (1981). *The Silent Language.* Garden City, NY: Anchor/Doubleday.

Handler, J.F. (1986). *The Conditions of Discretion: Autonomy, Community, Bureaucracy.* New York: Russell Sage Foundation.

Haque, A. (2004). Ethics and administrative discretion in a unified administration. *Administration & Society,* 35, 701–716.

Harmon, M.T., & Mayer, R.T. (1986). *Organization Theory for Public Administration.* New York: Little, Brown.

Heath, R.L. (2001). *Handbook of Public Relations.* Thousand Oaks, CA: Sage.

Herron, S. (2001). Dealing with the aftermath: Stress management for critical-incident responders. *Sheriff,* 53, 36–37.

Hertenstein, M.J., & Keltner, D. (2010). Gender and the communication of emotion via touch. *Sex Roles,* 63, 1–11.

Hess, U., Senecal, S., Kirouac, G., Herrera, P., Philippot, P., & Kleck, R.E. (2000). Emotional expressivity in men and women: Stereotypes and self-perceptions. *Cognition and Emotion,* 14, 609–642.

Hickson, M., III, Stacks, D.W., & Moore, N. (2004). *Nonverbal Communication: Studies and Applications,* 4th ed. Los Angeles: Roxbury.

Hiebert, R.E., & Spitzer, C.E. (1968). *The Voice of Government.* New York: John Wiley.

Hobbes, T. (1651/1958). *Leviathan: Parts One and Two.* New York, NY: Macmillan Publishing Company.

Hochschild, A.R. (1979). Emotion work, feeling rules, and social structure. *American Journal of Sociology,* 85, 551–575.

———. (1983). *The Managed Heart: Commercialization of Human Feeling.* Berkeley: University of California Press.

Holmes, O.W., Sr. (1858). *The Autocrat of the Breakfast Table: A Collection of Essays.* Boston: Phillips, Sampson.

Hsieh, A.T., & Hsieh, S.H. (2010). Dangerous work and name disclosure. *Journal of Criminal Justice*, 38, 410–418.

Hsieh, C.W. (2009). Emotional labor in public service roles: A model of dramaturgical and dispositional approaches. Doctoral dissertation, Florida State University. http://etd.lib.fsu.edu/theses/available/etd-07092009-182534/.

Hsieh, C.W., & Guy, M.E. (2009). Performance outcomes: The relationship between managing the "heart" and managing client satisfaction. *Review of Public Personnel Administration*, 29, 41–57.

Hsieh, C.W., Jin, M., & Guy, M.E. (2011). Consequences of work-related emotions: Analysis of a cross section of public service workers. *American Review of Public Administration*. First published February 21, 2011 (DOI:10.1177/0275074010896078.)

Illinois Department of Transportation (IDOT). (2009). Average daily total traffic: State primary system, Illinois, Chicago and vicinity. www.dot.state.il.us/trafficmaps/ADT_chicago.pdf.

Ink, D. (2006). An analysis of the House Select Committee and White House reports on Hurricane Katrina. *Public Administration Review*, 66, 800–807.

Izard, C.E. (1992). Basic emotions, relations among emotions, and emotion-cognition relations. *Psychological Review*, 99, 561–565.

Janis, I.L., & Mann, L. (1977). *Decision Making.* New York: Free Press.

Jarret, J. (2007). Maintaining your credibility in a crisis: Challenges for the manager. *Public Management,* April, 14–16.

Jin, M., & Guy, M.E. (2009). The connection between performance management and emotional labor: An examination of consumer complaint workers. *Public Performance and Management Review*, 33, 83–100.

Johnson, H.A.M. (2007). Service with a smile: Antecedents and consequences of emotional labor strategies. Doctoral dissertation, University of South Florida.

Jones, W.H.M. (1957). *India's Parliament.* London: Allen and Unwin.

Kane, J., & Patapan, H. (2006). In search of prudence: The hidden problem of managerial reform. *Public Administration Review*, 66(5), 711–724.

Kapucu, N. (2003). Public sector reform in New Zealand: Transformation of the society. *Turkish Political Science and Public Administration Journal*, 58, 123–143.

Katz, D., & Kahn, R.L. (1978). *The Social Psychology of Organizations*, 2nd ed. New York: Wiley.

Kaufman, H. (1960). *The Forest Ranger: A Study in Administrative Behavior.* Baltimore, MD: Johns Hopkins University Press.

Kelly, C. (2010). On the eve of rescue, trapped miners get media training. *Toronto Star*, October 12. www.thestar.com/news/world/chile/article/873875—on-the-eve-of-rescue-trapped-miners-get-media-training?bn=1.

Kelly, M. (1994). Theories of justice and street-level discretion. *Journal of Public Administration Research and Theory*, 4, 119–140.

Killenberg, G.M. (1992). *Public Affairs Reporting: Covering the News in the Information Age.* New York: St. Martin's Press.

Koontz, T. (2007). Federal and state public forest administration in the new millennium: Revisiting Herbert Kaufman's "The Forest Ranger." *Public Administration Review*, 67, 152–164.

Kovach, B., & Rosenthal, T. (1999). *Warp Speed: America in the Age of Mixed Media.* New York: Century Foundation Press.

Kring, A.M., & Gordon, A.H. (1998). Sex differences in emotion: Expression, experience, and physiology. *Journal of Personality and Social Psychology,* 74, 686–703.

Krislov, S. (1974). *Representative Bureaucracy.* Englewood Cliffs, NJ: Prentice Hall.

Krislov, S., & Rosenbloom, D.H. 1981. *Representative Bureaucracy and the American Political System.* New York: Praeger.

Krugman, P. (2007). *The Conscience of a Liberal.* New York: Norton.

Laitin, J. (1980). Public information in government: Some contrasting views. *Management,* 2, 9–14.

Lee, M. (1999). Reporters and bureaucrats: Public relations counter-strategies by public administrators in an era of media disinterest in government. *Public Relations Review,* 25, 451–463.

———. (2001). The agency spokesperson: Connecting public administration and the media. *Public Administration Quarterly,* 25, 101–130.

Leigh, J.P. (1991). No evidence of compensating wages for occupational fatalities. *Industrial Relations,* 30, 382–395.

Lerbringer, O. (1977). *The Crisis Manager.* Mahwah, NJ: Lawrence Erlbaum.

Lewis, R.G. (1988). Management issues in emergency response. In *Managing Disaster: Strategies and Policy Perspectives,* ed. L.K. Comfort. Durham, NC: Duke University Press.

Lifton, R.J. (1986). *The Nazi Doctors: Medical Killing and the Psychology of Genocide.* New York: Basic Books.

Lipsky, M. (1983). *Street-Level Bureaucracy.* New York: Russell Sage Foundation.

Liska, H. (2010). Personal interview with author, December 14.

Liu, Y., Perrewe, P.L., Hochwarter, W.A., & Kacmar, C.J. (2004). Dispositional antecedents and consequences of emotional labor at work. *Journal of Leadership & Organizational Studies,* 10, 12–25.

Lopez, S.H. (2006). Emotional labor and organized emotional care: Conceptualizing nursing home care work. *Work & Occupations,* 33, 133–160.

Luke, C. (1999). Media and cultural studies in Australia. *Journal of Adolescent & Adult Literacy,* 42, 622–626.

Madrick, J. (2009). *The Case for Big Government.* Princeton, NJ: Princeton University Press.

Mastracci, S.H. (2004). *Breaking Out of the Pink-Collar Ghetto.* Armonk, NY: M.E. Sharpe.

Mastracci, S.H., Newman, M.A., & Guy, M.E. (2006). Appraising emotion work: Determining whether emotional labor is valued in government jobs. *American Review of Public Administration,* 36, 123–138.

———. (2009). Emotional labor: How to teach it, why to teach it. *Journal of Public Affairs Education,* 16, 123–141.

Mayer, J.D., & Salovey, P. (1993). The intelligence of emotional intelligence. *Intelligence,* 17, 433–443.

Maynard-Moody, S.W., & Leland, S. (2000). Stories from the front lines of public management: Street level workers as responsible actors. In *Advancing Public Management: New Developments in Theory, Methods, and Practice,* ed. H. Rainey & J. Brudney. Washington, DC: Georgetown University Press.

Maynard-Moody, S.W., & Musheno, M.C. (2000). State agent or citizen agent: Two narratives of discretion. *Journal of Public Administration Research and Theory*, 10, 329–358.

———. (2003). *Cops, Teachers, Counselors: Stories from the Front Lines of Public Service*. Ann Arbor: University of Michigan Press.

McCloskey, D.N. (1996). *The Vices of Economists—The Virtues of the Bourgeoisie*. Amsterdam, Netherlands: Amsterdam University Press.

———. Lingonomics: Thoughts and theorems about the role of language in the economy. Unpublished manuscript presented before the University of Illinois at Chicago economics department seminar, September 18.

McCroskey, J.C. (1998). *An Introduction to Communication in the Classroom*, 2nd ed. Acton, MA: Tapestry Press.

Mehrabian, A. (2007). *Nonverbal communication*. New Brunswick, NJ: Aldine-Atherton.

Meng, R., & Smith, D.A. (1999). The impact of workers' compensation on wage premiums for job hazards. *Applied Economics*, 31, 1101–1108.

Milbank, D. (2010). Obama's oil spill response: Too much culpability, too much passivity. *Washington Post*, May 30.

Mitchell, J.T. (1988). The impact of stress on emergency service personnel: Policy issues in emergency response. In *Managing Disaster: Strategies and Policy Perspectives*, ed. L.K. Comfort. Durham, NC: Duke University Press.

Moltoch, H. (2006). Death on the roof: Race and bureaucratic failure. *Space and Culture*, 9, 31–34.

Moore, M.J., & Viscusi, W.K. (1990). Models for estimating discount rates for long-term health risks using labor market data. *Journal of Risk and Uncertainty*, 3, 381–401.

Morgan, D. (1986). *The Flacks of Washington: Government Information and the Public Agenda*. New York: Greenwood Press.

Naff, K.C., & Crum, J. (1999). Working for America: Does public service motivation make a difference? *Review of Public Personnel Administration*, 19, 5–16.

Nagel, J.H. (1991). Psychological obstacles to administrative responsibility: Lessons of the MOVE disaster. *Journal of Policy Analysis and Management*, 10, 1–23.

National Academy of Public Administration (NAPA). (1993). *Coping with Catastrophe. Building an Emergency Management System to Meet People's Needs in Natural and Manmade Disasters*. U.S. Congress and Federal Emergency Management Agency.

Newman, M.A., Guy, M.E., & Mastracci, S.H. (2009). Beyond cognition: Affective leadership and emotional labor. *Public Administration Review*, 69, 6–20.

Nozick, R. (1974). *Anarchy, State, and Utopia*. Cambridge, MA: Harvard University Press.

Olson, C.A. (1981). An analysis of wage differentials received by workers on dangerous jobs. *Journal of Human Resources*, 16, 167–185.

Opengart, R. (2005). Emotional intelligence and emotion work: Examining constructs from an interdisciplinary framework. *Human Resource Development Review*, 4(1), 49–62.

Parsons, T., & Shils, E. (1951). *Toward a General Theory of Action*. Cambridge, MA: Harvard University Press.

Patterson, K, Grenny, J., McMillan, R. & Switzler, A. (2002). *Crucial Conversations: Tools for Talking When Stakes Are High.* New York: McGraw-Hill.

Peck, J., and Theodore, N. (2002). Work first: Workfare and the regulation of contingent labor markets. *Cambridge Journal of Economics*, 24, 119–138.

Perry, J.L. (1996). Measuring public service motivation: An assessment of construct reliability and validity. *Journal of Public Administration Research and Theory*, 6, 5–22.

———. (1997). Antecedents of public service motivation. *Journal of Public Administration Research and Theory*, 7, 181–197.

Perry, J.L., & Wise, L.R. (1990). The motivational bases of public service. *Public Administration Review*, 50, 367–373.

Phelps, C. (2010). Personal interview with author, June 14.

Phillips, S.W., & Sobel, J.J. (2010). Twenty years of mandatory arrest: Police decision making in the face of legal requirements. *Criminal Justice Policy Review*, 21, 98–118.

Pielke, R.A., Jr., Gratz, J., Landsea, C.W., Collins, D., Saunders, M.A., & Musulin, R. (2008). Normalized hurricane damage in the United States: 1900–2005. *Natural Hazards Review*, 9, 29–42.

Pijnenburg, B., & van Duin, M. (1991). The Zeebrugge ferry disaster: Elements of a communication and information processes scenario. In *Crisis Management and Decision Making: Simulation Oriented Scenarios*, ed. U. Rosenthal & B. Pijnenburg. Dordrecht, Netherlands: Kluwer Academic.

Pogrebin, M.R., & Poole, E.D. (1991). Police and tragic events: The management of emotions. *Journal of Criminal Justice*, 19, 395–403.

Pohl, G.M., & Vandeventer, D. (2001). The workplace, undergraduate education, and career preparation: The public relations academic and practitioner views. In *Handbook of Public Relations*, ed. R.L. Heath. Thousand Oaks, CA: Sage.

Preib, M. (2010). *The Wagon and Other Stories from the City.* Chicago: University of Chicago Press.

Rafaeli, A. (1989). When clerks meet customers: A test of variables related to emotional expressions on the job. *Journal of Applied Psychology*, 74, 385–393.

Rafaeli, A., & Sutton, R.I. (1988). The expression of emotion as part of the work role. *Academy of Management Review*, 12, 23–37.

Rahim, M.A., & Buntzman, G.F. (1991). Impression management and organizational conflict. In *Applied Impression Management: How Image-Making Affects Managerial Decisions*, ed. R.A. Giacaione & P. Rosenfeld. Newbury Park, CA: Sage.

Rawls, J. (1971). *A Theory of Justice.* Cambridge, MA: Harvard University Press.

Richards, J.M., & Gross, J.J. (1999). Composure at any cost? The cognitive consequences of emotion suppression. *Personality and Social Psychology Bulletin*, 25, 1033–1044.

Rietti, S. (2009). Emotion work and the philosophy of emotion. *Journal of Social Philosophy*, 40, 55–74.

Roberts, J.T. (1982). *Accountability in Athenian Government.* Madison: University of Wisconsin Press.

Rockman, B.A. (1998). The changing role of the state. In *Taking Stock: Assessing Public Sector Reforms*, ed. B.G. Peters & D.J. Savoie. Montreal, Canada: McGill-Queen's University Press.

Romzek, B.S. (2000). Dynamics of public sector accountability in an era of reform. *International Review of Administrative Sciences*, 66, 21–44.

Romzek, B.S., & Dubnick, M.J. (1987). Accountability in the public sector: Lessons from the Challenger tragedy. *Public Administration Review*, 47, 227–238.

————. (1998). Accountability. In *International Encyclopedia of Public Policy and Administration*, ed. J.M. Shafritz. Boulder, CO: Westview Press.

Rosenfeld, P., & Giacalone, R.A. (1991). From extreme to mainstream: Applied impression management in organizations. In *Applied Impression Management: How Image-Making Affects Managerial Decisions*, ed. R.A. Giacaione & P. Rosenfeld. Newbury Park, CA: Sage.

Rosenthal, U., Charles, M.T., & Hart, P.T. (1989). *Coping with Crises: The Management of Disasters, Riots and Terrorism*. Springfield, IL: Charles C. Thomas.

Salovey, P., & Mayer, J.D. (1990). Emotional intelligence. *Imagination, Cognition, and Personality*, 9, 185–211.

Schartau, P.E.S., Dalgleish, T., & Dunn, B.D. (2009). Seeing the bigger picture: Training in perspective broadening reduces self-reported affect and psychological response to distressing films and autobiographical memories. *Journal of Abnormal Psychology*, 118, 15–27.

Schaubroeck, J., & Jones, J.R. (2000). Antecedents of workplace emotional labor dimensions and moderators of their effects on physical symptoms. *Journal of Organizational Behavior*, 21, 163–183.

Scheibe, S., & Blanchard-Fields, F. (2009). Effects of regulating emotions on cognitive performance: What is costly for young adults is not so costly for older adults. *Psychology and Aging*, 24, 217–223.

Schmeichel, B.J. (2007). Attention control, memory updating and emotion regulation temporarily reduce the capacity for executive control. *Journal of Experimental Psychology: General*, 136, 241–255.

Schmeichel, B.J., Volokhov, R.N., & Demaree, H.A. (2008). Working memory capacity and the self-regulation of emotional expression and experience. *Journal of Personality and Social Psychology*, 95, 1526–1540.

Schmitt, J.F. (1994). *Mastering Tactics: A Tactical Decision Game Workbook*. Quantico, VA: United States Marine Corps Association.

Schneider, S.K. (1992). Governmental response to disasters: The conflict between bureaucratic procedures and emergent norms. *Public Administration Review*, 52, 135–145.

Schwartz, R., & Sulitzeanu-Kenan, R. (2004). Managerial values and accountability pressures: Challenges of crisis and disaster. *Journal of Public Administration Research and Theory*, 14, 79–102.

Scott, P.G. (1997). Assessing determinants of bureaucratic discretion: An experiment in street-level decision making. *Journal of Public Administration Research and Theory*, 7, 35–57.

Seeger, M., Sellnow, T., & Ulmer, R. (2001). Public relations and crisis communication: Organizing and chaos. In *Handbook of Public Relations*, ed. R.R. Heath. Thousand Oaks, CA: Sage.

Shields, S.A., & Koster, B.A. (1989). Emotional stereotyping in child rearing manuals, 1915–1980. *Social Psychology Quarterly*, 52, 44–55.

Simon, H.A. (1997). *Administrative Behavior: A Study of Decision Making Processes in Administrative Organizations*, 4th ed. New York: Free Press.

Simon, R.W., & Nath, L.E. (2004). Gender and emotion in the United States: Do men and women differ in self-reports of feelings and expressive behavior? *American Journal of Sociology*, 109, 1137–1176.

Skocpol, T. (1992). State formation and social policy in the United States. *American Behavioral Scientist*, 35, 559–584.

Smith, A. (1776/1991). *The Wealth of Nations*. New York: Prometheus Books (reprint).

Sowa, J.E., & Selden, S.C. (2003). Administrative discretion and active representation: An expansion of the theory of representative bureaucracy. *Public Administration Review*, 63, 700–709.

Stamm, B.H. (2008). Professional quality of life (ProQOL) questionnaire. www.proqol.org.

Steinbeck, J. (1939). *The Grapes of Wrath*. New York: Viking Press.

Stivers, C.M. (1994). The listening bureaucrat: Responsiveness in public administration. *Public Administration Review*, 54, 364–369.

Stivers, C.M. (2007). So poor and so black: Hurricane Katrina, public administration, and the issue of race. *Public Administration Review*, 67, 48–56.

Stivers, C.M. (2008). *Governance in Dark Times: Practical Philosophy for Public Administration*. Washington, DC: Georgetown University Press.

Stone, B. (1995). Administrative accountability in the Westminster democracies: Towards a new conceptual framework. *Governance*, 8, 505–526.

Sylves, R.T., & Waugh, W.L. (1990). *Cities and Disaster: North American Studies in Emergency Management*. Springfield, IL: Charles C. Thomas.

Taylor, F.W. (1911/1997). Scientific management. In *Classics of Public Administration*, 4th ed., ed. J.M. Shafritz & A.C. Hyde, pp. 43–46. Fort Worth, TX: Harcourt Brace.

Thomas, P.G. (1998). The changing nature of accountability. In *Taking Stock: Assessing Public Sector Reforms*, ed. B.G. Peters & D.J. Savoie, pp. 348–393. Montreal, Canada: McGill-Queen's University Press.

Thompson, F.J. (1982). Bureaucratic discretion and the National Health Service Corps. *Political Science Quarterly*, 97, 427–445.

Troxell, R.M. (2008). Indirect exposure to the trauma of others: The experiences of 911 telecommunicators. Doctoral dissertation, University of Illinois at Chicago.

Truman, D.B. (1951). *The Governmental Process: Political Interests and Public Opinion*. New York: Knopf.

Vinzant, J.C., & Crothers, L. (1998). *Street-Level Leadership: Discretion and Legitimacy in Front-Line Public Service*. Washington, DC: Georgetown University Press.

Viscusi, W.K. (1978). Wealth effects and earnings premiums for job hazards. *Review of Economics and Statistics*, 60, 408–416.

Viscusi, W.K. (1992). *Fatal Tradeoffs: Public and Private Responsibilities for Risk*. New York: Oxford University Press.

Viteritti, J.P. (1997). The environmental context of communication: Public sector organizations. In *Handbook of Administrative Communication*, ed. J.L. Garnett & A. Kouzmin. New York: Marcel Dekker.

Waldo, Dwight, (1992). "Foreword," in James L. Garnett, *Communicating for Results in Government: A Strategic Approach for Public Managers*. San Francisco: Jossey-Bass.

Waugh, W.L. (1988). Current policy and implementation issues in disaster preparedness. In *Managing Disaster: Strategies and Policy Perspectives*, ed. L.K. Comfort. Durham, NC: Duke University Press.

Weber, M. (1922/1997). Bureaucracy. In *Classics of Public Administration*, 4th ed., ed. J.M. Shafritz & A.C. Hyde, pp. 50–56. Fort Worth, TX: Harcourt Brace.

Welch, M. (2005). They shoot helicopters, don't they? How journalists spread rumors during Katrina. *Reason*, December. http://reason.com/issues/december-2005.

Wharton, A.S. (2009). The sociology of emotional labor. *Annual Review of Sociology*, 35, 147–165.

Wharton, A.S., & Erickson, R.J. (1995). The consequences of caring: Exploring the links between women's job and family emotion work. *Sociological Quarterly*, 36, 273–297.

Wong, C.S., & Law, K.S. (2002). The effects of leader and follower emotional intelligence on performance and attitude: An exploratory study. *Leadership Quarterly*, 13, 243–274.

Yanow, D., & Schwartz-Shea, P. (2006). *Interpretation and Method: Empirical Research Methods and the Interpretive Turn*. Armonk, NY: M.E. Sharpe.

Zorthian, B. (1970). Effective press relations. *Marine Corps Gazette*, 54, 36–42.

Index

About the Authors

Sharon H. Mastracci is an associate professor at the University of Illinois at Chicago. She conducts research in human resource management and employment policy and has been published in a wide range of publications, from *Policy Studies Journal* to *Public Voices*. She received the Rita Mae Kelly award for outstanding research on women's issues. She also serves as chair of the Public Administration Section of the American Political Science Association.

Mary E. Guy is professor and director of the Master of Public Administration program for the School of Public Affairs at the University of Colorado Denver. Her research and teaching interests focus on the human processes involved in public service delivery, and she has published a number of books and articles on the subject. Her work has been honored by the American Society for Public Administration, the Academy of Management, the journal *Public Administration Review*, and by multiple faculty mentor awards. She is a Fellow of the National Academy of Public Administration, past president of the American Society for Public Administration, and past chair of the Commission on Peer Review and Accreditation.

Meredith A. Newman is professor and chair of the Department of Public Administration at Florida International University. Prior to her career in academia, Newman served with the Australian Department of Foreign Affairs (in France and Vietnam), the U.S. Department of State (in Senegal, Malaysia, and Singapore), and the World Bank. She is widely published in the areas of public management, human resources and gender, and the emotive aspects of work. She is the recipient of several awards, including the Editors' Choice Award, *Public Administration Review*. Newman is past chair of the Commission on Peer Review and Accreditation, vice president for North America, International Association of Schools and Institutes of Administration; immediate past president of the American Society for Public Administration; and a Fellow of the National Academy of Public Administration.